OVEN TO TABLE

Also by Jan Scott

Gatherings: Bringing People Together with Food (with Julie Van Rosendaal)

OVEN
TO
TABLE

OVER 100 ONE-POT AND **ONE-PAN**
RECIPES FOR YOUR SHEET PAN, SKILLET,
DUTCH OVEN, AND MORE

JAN SCOTT

PENGUIN

an imprint of Penguin Canada, a division of Penguin Random House Canada Limited

Canada • USA • UK • Ireland • Australia • New Zealand • India • South Africa • China

First published 2019

www.penguinrandomhouse.ca

LIBRARY AND ARCHIVES CANADA CATALOGUING IN PUBLICATION

Scott, Jan, 1976-, author
   Oven to table : over 100 one-pot and one-pan recipes for
your sheet pan, skillet, dutch oven, and more / Jan Scott.

Includes index.
Issued in print and electronic formats.
ISBN 978-0-7352-3449-9 (softcover).—ISBN 978-0-7352-3450-5 (electronic)

   1. One-dish meals. 2. Quick and easy cooking. 3. Cookbooks.
I. Title. II. Title: Over 100 one-pot and one-pan recipes for your sheet
pan, skillet, dutch oven, and more.

TX840.O53S32 2019   641.82   C2018-904243-5
                                           C2018-904244-3

Cover and interior design by Rachel Cooper
Cover and interior photography by Jan Scott
Food and prop styling by Jennifer Bartoli and Jan Scott

Printed and bound in China

10 9 8 7 6 5 4 3 2 1

Penguin
Random House
PENGUIN CANADA

For Rob.
Without you, this book wouldn't
have been possible.
Thank you.

CONTENTS

ONE PAN, MANY POSSIBILITIES

This book couldn't come at a better time. With an increase in obligations and digital distractions that tempt us away from the kitchen, a healthy, home-cooked meal is one of the sacrifices many are making. Fortunately, there's a satisfying solution to help home cooks make stress-free, mess-free, and tasty meals a reality: one-pot or one-pan cooking.

The roots of cooking, from both an anthropological point of view as well as a personal one, began in one pot. Although scientists continue to hotly debate which group of people first mastered fire, it only stands to reason that they cooked most of what they ate in one pot simply because so few other tools were available. In my own starter kitchen—a small and ill-equipped one at that—it never occurred to me to own multiple cooking vessels. My student budget was tight and supplies were limited, but that didn't stop me from dishing up grub to tables full of friends and fellow housemates. Today, I rely heavily on one-pot cooking for its convenience in helping me feed my brood of boys. With a husband and three sons at my table, all of whom unquestionably eat more than three times a day, making a meal in just one pot is what saves my sanity, not to mention my time.

Of course, families aren't the only ones in need of these simplified cooking methods. My mom is a single working woman with a ninety-minute commute each day. Her commitment to eating well is reinforced when she can get dinner on the table in a timely manner. Not to mention, one-pot cooking lends itself well to a speedy cleanup, as fewer dishes inevitably crowd the kitchen sink. My oldest son—soon to be a university student in charge of making most of his own meals—is a devout one-pot cook, because goodness knows if he had to rely on multiple cooking vessels to get food into him, he'd likely be living off of PB&Js for the next four to eight years. And let's not forget about newlyweds and empty nesters, two demographics potentially also in need of mealtime simplification. One group is likely busy building their careers and has limited time for complex daily cooking projects, while the other group could be ready to scale back the amount of time they spend in the kitchen after decades of nightly meal making.

Using one of six groups of cooking vessels—skillets, sheet pans, Dutch ovens, everyday baking pans, enamel roasting pans, and stoneware casserole dishes—my one-pot creations are designed to bring a complete dish to the table using easy-to-source ingredients and a variety of foolproof cooking techniques. From stir-fries to stews and cobblers to casseroles, this collection of down-to-earth recipes brings ease, comfort, and bold flavours to everyday home cooking. Flexible and endlessly adaptable, preparing food in one pot not only saves time, both in the prep and post-meal cleanup, but also allows for smart seasonal cooking. The dishes included in this book are prepared or served in a single pot, pan, skillet, or casserole dish and emphasize the versatility that can be created with just a few pieces of humble cookware.

Speaking of cookware, the good news here is that you probably have most of these items in your kitchen cabinets already. Oven-to-table pieces like Dutch ovens, sheet pans, skillets, and casserole dishes are essential when it comes to feeding a busy family or hosting a gathering. Roasting pans, while perhaps less common, should be considered essential, as they are practical for so much more than roasts. They can be used to bake French toast or roast a complete chicken dinner, and they lend themselves well to cooking a variety of side dishes. Not only do most of us not have enough space to store the pots and pans we need for cooking plus an additional set of dishes for serving food, it can be a hassle to transfer everything just to make the table look fancy. Instead, these pieces are ready to leap from stove to centrepiece in an instant. Most of these items are just as comfortable on the daily dinner table as they are at a holiday feast, and these recipes will not only streamline the meals you make, but also satiate the people you share them with.

My hope is that *Oven to Table* will show less experienced cooks just how easy it is to create simple, wholesome meals, while inspiring more seasoned ones to try their hand at new recipes and simplified techniques. Uncomplicated food can be the best to eat, the most fun to share, and certainly the most enjoyable to cook.

TRADITIONAL COOKWARE
IN THE MODERN KITCHEN

Each of the traditional cooking vessels used in this book is rich with culinary history, yet remains perfectly at place in the modern home kitchen. Cooking in one pot or pan means leaning on those time-honoured pieces that have stood the test of time and proven their worth. A solid pot and durable pan are versatile and worth the storage space (not to mention the financial invest-ment), and will afford you the opportunity to cook almost anything. Don't worry: I'm not suggesting you run out and purchase everything on this list before cooking; in fact, I firmly believe in the opposite. Collect the pieces over time, adding to your kitchenware arsenal as you master the basics. I would start with an inexpensive sheet pan and multi-purpose Dutch oven and build up your collection from there.

DUTCH OVENS: These are undoubtedly the workhorses of my kitchen, and it's rare that there isn't a pot of soup (pages 52–67) simmering on the stovetop or a piece of meat braising in the oven, both of which can be done in one of these wonder pots. My recommendation is to own two: one medium and one large, if possible. Their price can vary depending on the brand, but some are known to last a lifetime and are worth the investment. I keep one of mine on the stovetop at all times, clean and ready to use, so when I walk into the kitchen the only thing I need to do is get the stove going. You can read more of my poetic waxing about this pot on page 44.

SHEET PANS: Sometimes referred to as baking pans or baking sheets, these rimmed, rectangular metal pans are inexpensive and adaptable. They're usually made out of metal or aluminum, and I tend to stay away from the ones with a non-stick coating. I regularly use mine, flat and fitted with a 1-inch (2.5 cm) rim, for granola (page 36), cookies (page 202), grilled cheese sandwiches (page 95), and complete "meat and potato" dinners (pages 129, 138). Cooking on a sheet pan lets your oven do most of the work, while you take care of other more important things, whether it's helping your kids with their homework or spending time with dinner party guests. Page 76 has more information about this kitchen workhorse.

SKILLETS: If I were forced to choose only one pan to own, it would be a cast iron skillet. I consider this an all-purpose vessel and use mine for making sandwiches, searing meats, and baking cornbread (page 83), cobblers, and skillet sweets (page 210). It glides smoothly from stovetop to oven to table and retains heat remarkably well, ensuring that your food stays warm, which is ideal when entertaining or serving food buffet style. New cast iron pans are readily available at most housewares stores for reasonable prices, or you can buy used ones at an antique or flea market and fix them so they're like new again. For those a little apprehensive about the use and maintenance of traditional cast iron, an enamel-coated cast iron, stainless steel, or non-stick skillet is a suitable substitute. There's more to be learned about skillets and how to use and clean them on page 115.

ENAMELWARE ROASTING PANS: I use my enamel roasting pan several times a week for everything from roasted veggies (pages 171, 179) to baked French toast (page 35) to roasted chicken (page 123). Its vintage look suits my table perfectly, it's a snap to clean thanks to its naturally non-stick material, and it's durable enough to be used outdoors for warm-weather entertaining. The only problem I have with these pans is that I do not own nearly enough of them. Learn more about them on page 194.

CASSEROLE DISHES: Shallow casserole dishes, often made from glass, ceramic, or stoneware, are the ideal vessels for gratins, casseroles (page 33) and crisps (page 223), and can also be used for serving dips (pages 236, 239) to a larger crowd. The variety of shapes and capacities will suit almost any baking, broiling, or roasting recipe, and it's easy to choose a colourful collection that will match the rest of your dinnerware. I like that they can almost always be tucked in the freezer safely, allowing me to make parts of my meal ahead of time. Turn to page 164 for more information on cooking with these common casserole dishes.

BAKING PANS: Available in a myriad of shapes and sizes, some baking pans are single-use and explicitly used for a sole purpose, while others are more versatile and multi-purpose. Usually made out of metal, tin, stainless steel, glass, silicone, or stone, the type of material used can have an effect on the overall cooking time and temperature of the dish. For the purpose of this book, I relied mostly on the standard metal kind, but of course there were some exceptions and each is clearly indicated within the recipes. Some of my favourite baking pans included in this book are square, rectangular, doughnut, springform, and loaf pans; muffin tins; and pie plates. See page 231 for the complete lowdown on these kitchen staples.

TWENTY TENETS FOR SUCCESSFUL ONE-POT COOKING

One-pot cooking boils down to this: put preferred ingredients into your chosen vessel, apply heat, and magically it all comes together. Seasonings and fresh herbs help to round out flavours, and in many cases the addition of salt, fat, or acid at the end of the cooking time brightens and binds them to each other. Of course, there are a few other tips and tricks you can incorporate to make this style of cooking easier and speedier and to ensure the success of your dish.

1. By far, the most important strategy in one-pot cooking—or, arguably, in any type of cooking—is to set your mise en place. This French culinary term literally means "putting in place" and suggests that you should wash, prepare, cut, chop, and measure all ingredients needed for a dish before you begin to cook.

2. Always take the time to read each recipe before you get under way. You don't want any surprises when it comes time to make your meal. For example, the Perfect Saucy Pulled Pork (page 134) needs to be cooked the day before you serve it, and my pizza dough (see page 104) requires twelve to eighteen hours in the refrigerator to rise.

3. I encourage you to choose the freshest and finest ingredients (think organic produce, fresh herbs, good quality cheeses, etc.) that your budget will allow; it will make a difference in the end result of a recipe. I tested some recipes with lower quality pastas and cheeses and the results were not as tempting as the ones made with superior versions.

4. Use a potato masher to crumble ground meats. Many recipes call for using the back of a wooden spoon, but you have to work hard to turn the meat into small, uniform pieces. A potato masher works much better and brings about the texture and size you're looking for.

5. When bringing a pot of water to a boil, cover it with a lid and the water will come to a boil quicker. It seems like a simple enough idea, but many people forget to do this and they spend much longer than necessary waiting for their water to boil.

6. Speaking of boiling, always leave the lid of your pot slightly ajar to prevent foamy spillovers onto your burners.

7. Before cutting chicken, beef, or bacon, place them in the freezer for ten to twenty minutes, or just until they start to firm up, to make for easier slicing.

8. As tempting as it is to toss all of the ingredients into a pot or pan and hope for the best, if you take the time to brown the meat before you add the other ingredients, you'll end up with a better tasting meal—even if the meat isn't fully seared but cooks just long enough to get a bit of colour.

9. When using a skillet, make sure the pan is properly preheated before cooking. This helps to maintain a steady temperature while cooking.

10. Make cleanup even easier by lining your rimmed sheet pans with parchment paper or aluminum foil. This will prevent you from having to scrape off and scour cooked-on foods. When the pan has cooled, simply remove the lining and give the pan a scrub with soap and warm water.

11. One-pot cooking lends itself well to batch cooking, allowing you to make more than you need and save the extras for another day. Many of the recipes in this book can easily be doubled, or even tripled, and stored for future use.

12. If you find that your soups, stews, sauces, and braised meats look a little greasy, toss a few ice cubes into the pot. The fat will quickly cling to the icy cold cube, and then can be easily discarded.

13. Become as familiar with your oven as you are with your own family members, because one that runs too hot or too cold or that has troublesome hot spots can ruin a meal (specifically those made on a sheet pan) in no time. Whether your oven is an older model fitted with an electric stovetop or a top-of-the-line gas range, it doesn't hurt to buy an inexpensive oven thermometer so you can be sure you're consistently cooking at the correct temperature. I keep one in my oven at all times.

14. A rimmed sheet pan can quickly double as a lid for a skillet that doesn't come with one. I use them all the time, especially for my oversize pans that were purchased without an accompanying cover.

15. Keeping the ingredients list short and flavourful is essential to one-pot cooking, otherwise the simplifying aspect of the recipe becomes void. To do this, I rely on heavy-hitting ingredients like tomato paste and super flavourful sauces like soy and hoisin. I also almost always use chicken broth in place of water for my cooking liquid and don't hesitate to incorporate canned beans, legumes, and tomatoes and frozen peas whenever possible.

16. Finishing a one-pan dish with a flourish delivers the best results, which is why almost every savoury recipe in *Oven to Table* includes a garnish or sauce. From chopped fresh herbs to a squeeze of citrus to a simple drizzle of yogurt or sour cream, these final touches elevate both the taste and the look of a dish.

17. I often prep the vegetable component of my one-pot recipes in advance. Over the weekend, I like to wash, peel, and chop what I need for the week ahead so that the vegetables are ready for me when it's time to cook. Root and cruciferous vegetables can be prepped up to five days in advance and stored in an airtight container. I find that peppers tend to turn slimy if they are cut more than two or three days ahead of time. I prefer to cut softer veggies like tomatoes and zucchini just before using, though they will hold up for a day.

18. For particularly busy nights, I like to assemble a sheet pan meal early in the day, cover it with plastic wrap, and store the tray in the refrigerator until I'm ready to start cooking. I let everything come to room temperature while the oven preheats, and then slide the pan into the hot oven. It feels almost effortless to get a good meal on the table this way. Be careful to choose vegetables that can handle hanging out in the fridge for six to eight hours (root and cruciferous vegetables). Save chopping the softer ones (tomatoes and zucchini) until just before needed, if you can, but if not, prep those ones no more than a day in advance. If you're worried about the vegetables drying out on the sheet pan, tossing them with a light coating of olive oil will prevent that from happening.

19. Recipes are only guidelines—a road map of sorts to help you get where you need to go. Feel free to detour and replace one ingredient for another with similar traits. Swap in thyme for rosemary if that's what you prefer, or use black beans in place of kidney beans if you enjoy their taste more. Taking such liberties will allow you to create a whole new dish, expanding your one-pot recipe repertoire.

20. Cast iron skillets can be cleaned with soap! Conventional wisdom would have home cooks believe otherwise, but it's true. A quick swish of soap won't harm the seasoned surface, but a long soak will. Use the least aggressive cleaning method required to scour the pan, but don't live in fear of using soap. I cover this topic further in Skillet 101 on page 115.

COOKING TOOLBOX

There is no denying that some tools are more helpful than others when it comes to cooking in one pot. When you limit the number of vessels used to create a dish, it often forces you to rely on other kitchen gadgets to get the job done. I live in a tiny urban home with an even smaller space in which to cook, so if I'm suggesting you free up some precious counter and cupboard real estate for these items, you know they are definitely worth owning. Some are considered big investments, while others are more common and likely can be found in the drawer of most home cooks.

OVEN THERMOMETER: This indispensable device is essential to ensuring the success of a dish. Keep one in your oven at all times and use it regularly to guarantee that your oven is cooking food at the correct temperature. Another bonus is that it will let you know if your oven preheats in the amount of time it's supposed to. My oven thermometer showed me that when I preheat my oven to 425°F (220°C), it actually takes 10 minutes longer than the oven would have me believe to achieve that level of high heat. Most reliable models can be purchased for under $20.

FOOD PROCESSOR: A time saver for cutting and chopping, my food processor has a permanent place in my kitchen. Food processors vary in price, but many are of comparable quality, so you can get away with a less expensive model if that's what works best for your budget. I'm fond of my large Cuisinart model and use it for everything from making dips to cutting vegetables to binding ingredients together for baking.

THIN, FLEXIBLE METAL SPATULA: I adore this tool and use it nearly every day. For so much more than just fish—what this spatula is usually known for—this short-handled metal flipper has large slots cut out of it and an angled, bevelled edge, making it perfect for flipping practically everything. It seamlessly slides under food without catching it and can handle the heft of a half-pound hamburger just as easily as a delicate piece of fish or a pancake. I like the look of a wooden-handled spatula so I use one of those, but almost any will do. These are quite inexpensive, usually costing under $20.

PARCHMENT PAPER: Available in bleached and unbleached versions, this non-stick baking paper is the perfect liner for sheet pans when roasting vegetables, baking cookies, and cooking complete dinners. Most brands are oven safe up to 425°F (220°C), but I have used my parchment paper in ovens up to 450°F (230°C) without issue. Check the packaging of your favourite brand to verify.

A FEW FINE KNIVES: Good knives are essential for any home kitchen, especially ones where a lot of cooking gets done. Even though there is a separate knife for almost every kitchen task, you can easily get by with three of the most common ones: a chef's knife, a serrated or bread knife, and a paring knife. Nowadays, these knives are available in an array of styles, but look for the one that feels most comfortable in your hand. Also, be sure to invest in a knife sharpener; it will keep your hands safe and your knives in better working order.

CUTTING BOARD: Available in wood, plastic, and bamboo and priced at anywhere between $20 and $200, there are a lot of options when it comes to choosing a cutting board. I'm partial to wooden boards, but opt for ones that don't require too much handling (washing, drying, and oiling) to keep them in tip-top shape. I refuse to spend a small fortune on such boards, but do put a lot of stock into their proportions, which is why my everyday wooden cutting board measures roughly 15 × 20 inches (38 × 50 cm). If you use anything smaller, your chopped carrot coins are sure to roll right off the side, and spatchcocking a chicken would be practically impossible. To stabilize a cutting board, place a wet paper towel or thin damp cloth underneath it.

KITCHEN SHEARS: Essential for removing the backbone from a whole chicken or effortlessly slicing food (yes, skip the pizza cutter!), I keep a pair of kitchen shears on my counter and use them frequently enough to justify the small amount of real estate they take up in my tiny kitchen.

WIRE RACKS: Primarily used for cooling cookies and cakes, a wire cooling rack also comes in handy when making crispier baked foods. For example, in the Crispy Chicken Sandwiches (page 96), the wire rack suspends the breaded chicken, separating it from juices and fat, dramatically upping the crunch factor. Look for a rectangular metal rack (because these racks aren't specifically designed for the oven, any non-stick coatings may come off when heated and potentially ruin food) with a criss-cross pattern instead of metal slots. This will prevent food from slipping through and also allow for better air circulation. Look for a rack that fits snugly on your sheet pan, as you don't want it to slide around too much.

FINE MESH SIEVE: I recommend rinsing canned beans, lentils and legumes, and grains such as quinoa and farro before cooking, and this tool lets me do so easily. It washes well, stores easily, and can also be used to sift baking ingredients like flour, cocoa powder, and powdered sugar. Sieves are relatively inexpensive and can be found in most houseware, big box, or kitchen supply stores.

KITCHEN SCALE: Inexpensive and long lasting—I've had mine for thirteen years and have replaced the battery only once—every home kitchen should be outfitted with a digital kitchen scale. I use mine for weighing meats and vegetables, in baking, and to properly portion out food.

Other items I love to have on hand, but that aren't specific to one-pot cooking include:

MANUAL CITRUS JUICER: An inverted press makes quick work of extracting every last drop of juice from halved lemons, limes, and small oranges.

IMMERSION BLENDER: It's worth investing in an immersion blender if you make a lot of puréed soups or small batches of salad dressings, pesto, baby food, or smoothies. I like to use mine to make my hot drinks thick and frothy.

MICROPLANE GRATER: I can be a lazy cook, so instead of chopping or mincing garlic and ginger, you'll see I almost always call for it to be grated, and this is my tool of choice for such tasks. I also use it regularly to grate cheese, chocolate, and citrus peel and keep a miniature version on hand for grating fresh, whole spices like nutmeg.

PASTRY BRUSH: This kitchen paintbrush seems slightly useless for anything other than brushing egg wash over pastry, but in truth it's capable of so much more. I use it for basting meat, brushing butter and oil over skillets, and adding glazes. I also use one to clean my coffee grinder and to salvage every last bit of lemon zest from my microplane grater. Traditional pastry brushes sport bristles, and in my experience most of them are prone to shedding at some point. Modern pastry brushes are made of silicone, and while they are easier to clean they don't hold liquid all that well or coat food as evenly. I keep both types on hand and use one or the other depending on the task at hand.

TONGS: Kitchen tongs are essential for moving, turning, and rotating food with delicate precision. They can also be used to mix stir-fries, toss salads, and hold a piece of meat in place if you don't have a carving fork readily available (tongs won't puncture the meat). In truth, I use mine most frequently for grabbing hard-to-reach items from above my kitchen cabinets, where I store a lot of my cooking equipment.

MORTAR AND PESTLE: Jamie Oliver convinced me that I needed a mortar and pestle, especially after I watched him grind spices and make pesto, salad dressings, and a variety of sauces in his. When I feel inspired to cook like an Italian nonna, I ditch my electronic cooking assistants and turn to this timeless tool. I also like to serve guacamole in mine. I don't have a molcajete (a traditional stone mortar and pestle often used for salsas, moles, and guacamoles), so my mortar and pestle doubles as a serving vessel.

PANTRY PREFERENCES

Making great-tasting food at home requires cooks to keep their cupboards, refrigerator, and freezer sufficiently stocked. With just a few staple ingredients you can be on your way to achieving a fuss-free meal. A well-rounded assortment of ingredients is akin to having a fast-food restaurant right in your own home: you'll be able to cook what you crave and get a good meal on the table almost effortlessly.

EVERYDAY PANTRY ITEMS

- canned beans and chickpeas
- canned crushed and diced tomatoes
- canned tuna
- coconut milk
- coffee (ground beans and instant espresso powder for baking)
- dried cranberries
- evaporated milk
- hot sauce
- lentils
- oats (old-fashioned rolled)
- olives
- pasta (assorted shapes and sizes)
- peanut butter
- pumpkin purée
- raisins
- rice (basmati, brown, long-grain, short-grain)
- salsa
- soy sauce (regular or tamari)
- sugar (brown sugar, cane sugar, coarse sugar, powdered sugar, white sugar, honey, maple syrup)
- sweetened condensed milk
- tea (black, green, rooibos)
- tomato paste
- Worcestershire sauce

OILS AND VINEGARS

- apple cider vinegar
- balsamic vinegar
- canola, safflower, sunflower, or other vegetable oil of choice
- coconut oil
- extra-virgin olive oil
- olive oil cooking spray
- red and white wine vinegars
- rice wine vinegar

HERBS AND SPICES

- basil
- bay leaves
- black peppercorns
- cardamom
- cayenne
- celery seed
- cinnamon sticks
- crushed red pepper flakes
- garlic powder
- ground cinnamon
- ground cumin
- ground ginger
- nutmeg (whole)
- oregano
- paprika
- salt (kosher and Maldon)
- smoked paprika
- star anise

NUTS AND SEEDS
(STORE IN FREEZER ONCE PACKAGE IS OPENED)

- almonds
- pecans
- pumpkin seeds
- sesame seeds
- sunflower seeds
- walnuts

MISCELLANEOUS FREEZER ITEMS

- bacon
- frozen corn kernels
- frozen peas

DAIRY

- 2% milk
- assorted cheeses (cheddar, cream cheese, Parmesan, ricotta)

- buttermilk
- half-and-half cream (10%)
- heavy cream (35%)
- plain Greek yogurt (I prefer full-fat varieties)
- plain yogurt (I prefer full-fat varieties)
- salted butter
- sour cream (I prefer full-fat varieties)
- unsalted butter

BAKING SUPPLIES
- baking powder
- baking soda
- cocoa powder
- cornstarch

- flours (all-purpose, spelt, whole wheat)
- semi-sweet chocolate (chips, chunks, bars)
- vanilla bean paste

MISCELLANEOUS REFRIGERATOR ITEMS
- Dijon and whole grain mustard
- eggs
- fresh herbs (chives, cilantro, dill, parsley, rosemary, thyme)
- mayonnaise
- tahini sesame paste
- toasted sesame oil
- wonton wrappers

A BIT MORE ABOUT MY FAVOURITE PANTRY STAPLES

KOSHER SALT: This is my salt of choice and the kind I use in all recipes unless otherwise stated. I also like to keep sea salt on hand and usually use that for finishing a recipe. You'll notice that in most recipes I don't specify the amount of salt, instead allowing you, the cook, to determine how much you'd like to use. In my experience, each of us has our own personal preference when it comes to how salty we like our food, so why not get comfortable with seasoning your food for you? In some cases I have provided exact quantities; certain dishes really work best with specific amounts, especially if they contain other salty ingredients. Otherwise, taste frequently as you cook, and add a little salt at a time until you're happy with the flavour.

VANILLA BEAN PASTE: A convenient, affordable, flavourful, and versatile alternative to using whole vanilla beans, this is what I like to use in my cooking and baking. This natural, concentrated paste imparts a bold boost of vanilla flavour and mimics the appearance of whole vanilla bean seeds. Readily available in fine food, bulk food, and craft stores, you shouldn't have any trouble finding this where you live. If you prefer to use regular pure vanilla extract, please feel free.

MILK: Unless otherwise specified, I use 2% milk in my cooking and baking, but you can replace it with whatever suitable milk substitute you're fond of if you don't consume cow dairy. Just keep in mind that the flavour of almond and coconut milk may not complement what you're cooking, which is why it's important to be sure your alternative milk will work.

EGGS: I use standard large eggs in my cooking and baking recipes. Using a different size, without making an adjustment, will affect texture, flavour balance, and consistency in a recipe. To substitute another size, keep in mind that 1 large egg = 3 tablespoons (45 mL). You can also make an egg-free substitute for some recipes by combining 1 tablespoon (15 mL) ground flax or chia seeds with 2½ tablespoons (37 mL) water and letting the mixture rest for 5 to 15 minutes before proceeding with the recipe.

FLOURS: For the recipes in this book I've used all-purpose flour, whole wheat flour, and spelt flour, but you can substitute any of them with an appropriate gluten-free flour. There are many ways to measure flour, but I like this method (and it's the one I used when testing my recipes): aerate the flour with a fork or whisk, place the measuring cup into the bag or canister of flour, scoop the flour so it's heaping over the top of the cup, and then use the back of a knife to scrape across the top of the cup to level the flour. If you prefer to spoon the flour into the cup before levelling it off, that also works well.

A NOTE ABOUT THE RECIPES

- My goal with this book is to offer recipes for simple food with fresh flavours that appeal to eaters of all ages. It's written with the time-challenged or family-focused home cook in mind, and as such I try to use ingredients that should be readily available in most major supermarkets. Who wants to tote a toddler to three separate stores in search of something they may never find? If you see an ingredient listed that looks unfamiliar to you, rest assured it can be located in large chain grocery or bulk food stores.

- All of the recipes in this book are made entirely in one pot, pan, or dish, with only one exception. While researching, I discovered that most one-pot cookbooks actually call for the use of a few cooking vessels for each recipe—think one pot to boil water and one skillet to cook meat—but the final dish comes to the table in a single pan. I've strived to simplify that process even further and, as such, have created recipes that truly rely on just a single pot, pan, or dish for execution.

- In addition to keeping the cookware count low, I've also ensured that no recipe calls for more than three mixing bowls. While some recipes also require a food processor, blender, grater, or colander, you can be sure these are being used because they ultimately simplify the recipe, in terms of either speed or preparation.

- I almost always cook more than I need so I can keep a steady supply of leftovers in my fridge, and as such many of the recipes in this book serve between six and eight people. If you don't have that many mouths to feed, tuck the remains in the fridge for a week's worth of leftover lunches and gourmet breakfasts—the best "fast food" you'll ever eat.

- Every recipe includes a legend that classifies the dish based on a variety of dietary and cooking requirements:

VEGETARIAN: While the recipe may contain animal products, such as eggs, dairy, honey, etc., it does not contain any meat or fish.

GLUTEN-FREE: The recipe does not include any gluten, for those with celiac disease or gluten intolerance.

MAKE AHEAD: The recipe can be eaten and enjoyed as soon as it's ready, but will be just as tasty if you prepare it a day or two in advance and return to it when you're ready to eat. These recipes make great leftovers!

KID FRIENDLY: Based on my personal experience, the recipe is often a hit with children.

QUICK COOKING: Make the recipe in under 40 minutes from start to finish. These recipes are ideal for harried mornings, busy weeknights, or anytime you feel like getting a meal on the table in a timely manner.

WHOLE GRAIN: The recipe is made with mostly whole unprocessed grain.

BREAKFAST
AND BRUNCH

EVERYTHING THEY SAY about this important first meal of the day is true: eating breakfast will provide an energy boost, ward off mid-morning hunger pangs, and, perhaps most importantly, prevent unintentional crankiness early in the day. This is all well and good, but if you're someone who needs a bit more time to wake up and get going, the idea of making a meal the minute you roll out of bed probably doesn't hold a lot of appeal. When one can barely converse so early in the day, cooking feels downright impossible, and the easier it is to get food on the table, the better. One-pan breakfasts are the perfect weapon to combat fatigue and lethargy, and they lend them-selves just as well to early Monday mornings, such as with my Sheet Pan Breakfast with Sweet Potatoes and Chickpeas (page 30), as they do to slow and lazy weekends, when you can whip up a batch of Baked Oatmeal and Pear Breakfast Pie with Walnut Streusel Topping (page 22). They work well for feeding a crowd—try the Crowd-Pleasing Puffy Oven Pancake (page 25)— or simply a family of two, such as with my One-Pan English Breakfast (page 18), and in most cases the leftovers reheat wonderfully. Consider your mornings made.

ONE-PAN ENGLISH BREAKFAST

Serves 2

2 strips thick-cut bacon

2 pork breakfast sausages

½ small onion, cut into ¼-inch
(0.5 cm) thick slices

1 roma tomato, halved lengthwise and
seeded

4 cremini mushrooms, cleaned and
halved

1 can (14 ounces/398 mL) beans in
tomato sauce

2 large eggs

Kosher salt and freshly ground black
pepper

2 slices bread, toasted and buttered,
for serving (optional)

There are few nations that do breakfast better than Great Britain, and what gets included in a classic fry-up is a matter of region, not to mention personal taste. A combination of bacon and sausage is almost essential, as are eggs and beans. Speaking of beans, don't be afraid to reach for the canned kind here. They're classic, and the taste of the tinned sweet tomato sauce is hard to replicate at home. Having said that, if you have any Sweet and Saucy Baked Beans (page 191) left over in your fridge, they would definitely work well in a pinch. I like to use an enamel roasting pan for this dish, but a large cast iron skillet makes a suitable replacement.

1. Preheat the oven to 425°F (220°C). Place the bacon and sausages in a 9- × 13-inch (23 × 33 cm) enamel roasting pan and bake for 10 minutes.
2. Remove the pan from the oven and carefully transfer the bacon and sausages to a plate lined with paper towel. Cover with aluminum foil to keep warm. Place the onions, tomatoes, and mushrooms, cut side down, in a single layer in the pan. Return the baking pan to the oven and bake for another 10 minutes.
3. Flip the vegetables. Push the vegetables to one side of the pan and tip the beans into the other side of the pan. Create 2 wells anywhere in the pan. Crack an egg into each well and season with salt and pepper. Return the dish to the oven and bake for another 4 to 6 minutes or until the egg whites are set and yolks have reached the desired doneness.
4. Return the bacon and sausages to the pan. Serve immediately with toasted, buttered bread, if using.

SPICY CORN AND BACON FRITTATA

MAKE AHEAD, KID FRIENDLY,
QUICK COOKING, GLUTEN-FREE

Serves 4 to 6

A stir-and-bake Italian-style omelette, frittatas are easy, fast, and completely customizable. A good frittata should be equally at home on the breakfast, lunch, or dinner table and taste as good cold or at room temperature as it does hot. This particular variation hits these hallmarks easily, and also has the added benefit of being somewhat seasonless; prepare it in the summer when fresh corn is abundant (2 medium cobs should yield the correct amount) or in the winter with your favourite frozen variety.

1. Preheat the oven to 375°F (190°C).
2. In a 10-inch (25 cm) oven-safe cast iron, stainless steel, or non-stick skillet, cook the bacon until crisp, turning as needed, about 6 minutes. Transfer the bacon to a plate lined with paper towel, and drain all but 1 teaspoon (5 mL) of bacon fat from the skillet.
3. While the bacon is cooking, whisk together the eggs and ricotta cheese in a medium bowl until completely combined. Stir in ½ cup (125 mL) cheddar cheese and half the green onions, and season with salt and pepper.
4. Add the corn to the skillet and sauté until it softens, about 3 minutes. Chop the bacon and return to skillet. Stir in the jalapeños and combine thoroughly.
5. Pour the egg mixture over top and stir to combine with corn and bacon; sprinkle with the remaining ¼ cup (60 mL) cheddar cheese. Slide the skillet into the oven and bake for 12 to 15 minutes or until the eggs are set but not browned.
6. Remove the skillet from the oven and garnish with the remaining green onions and basil. Cut into wedges and serve immediately with the tomato sauce on the side.

4 strips thick-cut bacon

8 large eggs

½ cup (125 mL) full-fat, smooth ricotta cheese

¾ cup (175 mL) grated cheddar cheese, divided

2 green onions, white and light green parts only, thinly sliced, divided

Kosher salt

Freshly ground black pepper

1½ cups (375 mL) corn kernels (fresh or frozen)

3 tablespoons (45 mL) minced Quick Pickled Jalapeños (page 248) or store-bought

Fresh basil leaves, for garnish

1 cup (250 mL) spicy marinara or red pepper tomato sauce, warmed

BAKED OATMEAL AND PEAR BREAKFAST PIE WITH WALNUT STREUSEL TOPPING

Serves 6 to 8

For the oatmeal

¼ cup (60 mL) butter

3 cups (750 mL) old-fashioned rolled oats

½ cup (125 mL) packed brown sugar

½ teaspoon (2 mL) cinnamon

¼ teaspoon (1 mL) ground ginger

2 teaspoons (10 mL) baking powder

1 teaspoon (5 mL) kosher salt

2 cups (500 mL) milk (any kind)

2 large eggs

2 tablespoons (30 mL) maple syrup

1 teaspoon (5 mL) vanilla bean paste or pure vanilla extract

1 tablespoon (15 mL) finely grated orange zest (about 1 orange)

2 ripe pears, cored and diced, divided

For the streusel topping

½ cup (125 mL) all-purpose flour

6 tablespoons (90 mL) brown sugar

¼ cup (60 mL) butter, melted and cooled

6 tablespoons (90 mL) coarsely chopped walnuts

Pinch of salt

For serving

Plain or vanilla yogurt (optional)

Fresh pear slices (optional)

I love hot cereal in all its many forms, but I don't always have the minutes it takes to stand stove-side stirring a pot of grains, which is why this method of cooking them works perfectly. In the evening I assemble the short list of dry ingredients, and then in the morning I take care of the rest and let it bake while I wrestle the kids from their rooms. I think the scent of something warm and sweet wafting from the oven helps in getting family members downstairs. Unless you have a large family, this recipe makes enough for two mornings, which is even more reason to make it. Cooking once to eat twice is my favourite way to make anything. On the second day, just gently warm the oatmeal in the microwave or toaster oven and it will taste just as good. And just remember, baked oatmeal has the consistency of a moist cake rather than what you might expect from regular oatmeal.

1. Preheat the oven to 350°F (180°C). Place the butter in a 9-inch (23 cm) round deep-dish pie plate (or 8-inch/20 cm square baking pan) and slide it into the oven, letting the butter melt as the oven preheats.

2. In a medium mixing bowl, combine the oats, brown sugar, cinnamon, ginger, baking powder, and salt and stir well. In a second bowl or large glass measuring cup, whisk together the milk, eggs, maple syrup, vanilla, and orange zest.

3. Pour the wet ingredients into the dry ingredients and stir to combine. Fold in all but ½ cup (125 mL) of the diced pears. When the butter has melted (watch it closely to make sure it doesn't burn), remove the pie plate from the oven and add the oatmeal mixture, stirring it into the butter. Return to the oven and bake for 20 minutes or until the centre begins to set.

4. While the oatmeal is baking, prepare the streusel topping by mixing the flour, brown sugar, butter, walnuts, and salt in a small bowl with a fork. Remove the oatmeal from the oven, crumble the streusel topping over the oatmeal, scatter with the remaining ½ cup (125 mL) of diced pears, and return to the oven to bake until the centre of the oatmeal is set and the topping is golden brown, another 20 to 25 minutes. Cut into wedges and serve at once. Top with yogurt and fresh pear slices, if using.

CROWD-PLEASING
PUFFY OVEN PANCAKE

Serves 4 to 6

I've long loved the idea of a Dutch baby pancake, but have always found them too small to feed a crowd, or even a couple of teenage boys. This version, which we call a puffy oven pancake, is baked in a casserole dish instead of a skillet and delivers a properly portioned breakfast if you need to feed more than two or three people. Also known as a Dutch puff (and even a Hootin' Annie!), this pancake rises sky-high while baking but promptly flattens when it comes out of the oven, so gather your friends and family around to watch it deflate.

1. In the carafe of a blender, blend together the eggs, milk, flour, sugar, salt, and nutmeg. Let rest for 30 minutes.

2. Preheat the oven to 425°F (220°C). Place butter in a 9- × 13-inch (23 × 33 cm) casserole dish and slide it into the oven, letting the butter melt and bubble as the oven preheats.

3. When the butter has melted (watch it closely to make sure it doesn't burn), remove the pan from the oven and gently swirl the butter around to coat the sides and bottom of the dish. Blitz the batter for 10 seconds and pour it into the pan. Transfer to the oven quickly and close the door.

4. Bake for 20 minutes or until the puff is billowing over the sides of the pan and the edges are a dark golden brown. Quickly fill the centre with fresh berries, if using, and sprinkle with powdered sugar. Cut into squares and serve immediately with maple syrup for drizzling, if using.

5 large eggs, room temperature

1¼ cups (310 mL) whole milk

1¼ cups (310 mL) all-purpose flour

3 tablespoons (45 mL) granulated sugar

½ teaspoon (2 mL) salt

⅛ teaspoon (0.5 mL) freshly ground nutmeg

8 tablespoons (120 mL) butter

For serving

3 cups (750 mL) fresh berries (optional)

Powdered sugar

Maple syrup (optional)

EGG AND PANCETTA BISCUIT BAKE

Serves 6

1¾ cups (425 mL) all-purpose flour

¼ cup (60 mL) cornstarch

1 tablespoon (15 mL) baking powder

¼ teaspoon (1 mL) baking soda

¼ teaspoon (1 mL) kosher salt

½ teaspoon (2 mL) freshly ground
   black pepper, plus extra for
   seasoning

½ cup (125 mL) unsalted butter, chilled,
   plus extra for dish

1 cup + 2 tablespoons (280 mL)
   buttermilk

1 cup (250 mL) grated cheddar cheese,
   divided

1 cup (250 mL) diced pancetta

6 large eggs

6 cherry tomatoes, halved

2 green onions, trimmed and thinly
   sliced

It's hard not to love a good breakfast sandwich, and this biscuit bake is the one-pan version of that very thing. Instead of baking and splitting biscuits and filling them with fried eggs, I've found a way to make the entire thing in one casserole dish. Basic biscuit dough is pressed into a dish and topped with chopped pancetta, cheddar cheese, and eggs, which are cracked into small wells made with the back of a spoon. Cherry tomatoes and green onions add a healthy dose of colour to this hugely popular breakfast dish. Here's something to note: this dish is designed for those who don't mind a drippy egg yolk. If you cook the eggs until the yolks are firm, the biscuits tend to dry out a tad. While they are still delicious, you may find them to be a bit overcooked.

1. Preheat the oven to 425°F (220°C). Lightly butter an 11- × 7-inch (28 × 18 cm) enamel roasting pan and set aside.

2. In a medium bowl, whisk together the flour, cornstarch, baking powder, baking soda, salt, and pepper. Using the largest holes on a box grater, grate the butter into the dry ingredients. Use your fingers to work the butter into the flour, until the mixture resembles pea-size crumbles. Pour the buttermilk into the bowl and sprinkle with ⅔ cup (170 mL) of cheddar. Using a fork, gently stir the ingredients just until they come together to form a sticky, shaggy dough.

3. Scrape the dough into the prepared dish, pressing it evenly into the bottom and corners of the casserole dish. Sprinkle the biscuit dough with the remaining ⅓ cup (85 mL) of cheddar and the pancetta. Using the back of a large spoon, press down into the dough to create 6 deep wells. Crack an egg into each well and season with pepper.

4. Scatter the cherry tomato pieces around the eggs. Transfer the casserole dish to the oven and bake for 20 to 22 minutes or until the biscuit dough is golden brown along the edges, the egg whites are set, and the yolks have reached the desired doneness.

5. Remove the casserole dish from the oven and let cool for 5 minutes. Sprinkle with green onions, cut into 6 squares, and serve immediately.

GOAT CHEESE AND DILL
HASH BROWN QUICHE

VEGETARIAN, MAKE AHEAD, KID FRIENDLY,
GLUTEN-FREE

Serves 6 to 8

This quiche is in regular rotation at most of our brunch celebrations. The hash brown–style crust is a little lighter than traditional pastry and perfect for those with gluten sensitivities; the goat cheese and dill combination is simple yet continuously impresses. I especially love this dish because the crust can be made a day in advance. Store it covered in plastic wrap in the refrigerator overnight, and let it come to room temperature while the oven preheats before filling it.

1. Preheat the oven to 425°F (220°C). Brush the bottom and sides of a 9-inch (23 cm) pie plate or springform pan with some of the melted butter and set aside.
2. Using the largest holes on a box grater, shred the potatoes onto a clean dishtowel. Gather the ends of the towel together and thoroughly wring out the excess liquid into the sink. Transfer the potatoes to a medium mixing bowl and add the egg, remaining butter, salt, and pepper. Toss to combine. Press the potato mixture into the prepared pan with your fingers, covering the bottom and sides evenly.
3. Transfer the pie plate to the oven and bake until the potatoes are set and golden brown, 20 to 25 minutes. Remove the pie plate from the oven and let cool for 10 minutes. Reduce the oven heat to 350°F (180°C).
4. Using the same bowl from step 2 (give it a wipe with a piece of paper towel, if desired), whisk together the eggs, cream, goat cheese, dill, salt, and cayenne. Pour the egg mixture into the pie plate and season with black pepper. Bake for 40 to 45 minutes or until the centre of the quiche is set but soft, slightly puffed, and golden brown. Allow to cool for at least 15 minutes before serving.

VARIATION: Arrange approximately ½ pound (225 g) of asparagus (ends trimmed) on top of the quiche before baking.

For the crust

3 tablespoons (45 mL) butter, melted

2 large russet potatoes, peeled

1 large egg, lightly beaten

1 teaspoon (5 mL) kosher salt

½ teaspoon (2 mL) freshly ground
    black pepper

For the filling

6 large eggs

1¼ cups (310 mL) light (5%) cream

3 ounces (85 g) goat cheese

¼ cup (60 mL) chopped fresh dill,
    plus extra for garnish (optional)

½ teaspoon (2 mL) kosher salt

Pinch of cayenne pepper

Freshly ground black pepper

TIP: I find that the bottom crust best achieves the desired crispy, golden brown base when baked in a glass pie plate. While you can certainly use a ceramic or metal one if you prefer, note that the bottom of the quiche may not be as crisp as when cooked in glass.

SHEET PAN BREAKFAST WITH SWEET POTATOES AND CHICKPEAS

VEGETARIAN, KID FRIENDLY, QUICK COOKING, GLUTEN-FREE

Serves 2 to 4

1 can (19 ounces/540 mL) chickpeas, drained and rinsed

1 medium sweet potato, cut into ½-inch (1 cm) dice

3 tablespoons (45 mL) olive oil, divided

1 teaspoon (5 mL) smoked paprika

Kosher salt

4 large eggs

¼ teaspoon (1 mL) freshly ground black pepper

Chopped fresh chives, for garnish

Hot sauce, for serving (optional)

There's a lot to love about chickpeas, not the least of which is their versatility. These fibrous and protein-laden legumes shine at breakfast, and their wholesome makeup is sure to keep everyone feeling full until lunch. As an added bonus, the crunchy exterior they develop in the roasting process adds some welcome texture to this dish. Feel free to replace the sweet potatoes with Yukon Golds or russets, if you prefer.

1. Preheat the oven to 400°F (200°C). Spread the chickpeas on a clean kitchen towel and pat dry. On a rimmed sheet pan, combine the chickpeas, sweet potatoes, 2 tablespoons (30 mL) oil, paprika, and a pinch of salt. Toss to combine. Bake for 20 minutes, shaking the pan once halfway through the cooking time.

2. Remove the pan from the oven and make 4 wells among the chickpeas and sweet potatoes. Drizzle the remaining 1 tablespoon (15 mL) oil over each well. Crack an egg into each well and season with salt and pepper.

3. Bake for another 5 to 7 minutes or until the egg whites are set and yolks have reached the desired doneness. Sprinkle with chives and serve immediately with hot sauce on the side.

HAM AND CHEESE CROISSANT CASSEROLE

MAKE AHEAD, KID FRIENDLY

Serves 6

This is a breakfast casserole of the highest order, and while it leans a little in the direction of fancy, it really couldn't be easier to assemble. Day-old croissants are smeared with mustard, stuffed with grated Swiss and cheddar cheeses and deli-style ham, and nestled in a bed of garlicky egg custard. The flavours need time to develop and mingle, practically forcing you to make this ahead. Then simply bake the casserole the following day, impressing your family and friends with your early morning meal-making skills.

1. Lightly grease a 9- × 13-inch (23 × 33 cm) or similar-size casserole dish. In a small bowl, toss the cheeses together. Set aside.
2. Slice the croissants in half lengthwise and assemble the sandwiches by spreading each with 1 teaspoon (5 mL) mustard and filling with 2 slices of ham. Reserve ½ cup (125 mL) of the cheese and 1 tablespoon (15 mL) of the chives and evenly divide the remainder of each between the sandwiches. Close the sandwiches and layer them like shingles into the casserole dish, rounded edges pointing upward.
3. In a medium bowl, whisk together the eggs, milk, garlic, salt, and pepper. Pour the egg mixture evenly over the sandwiches, pressing the croissants firmly into the liquid. Sprinkle with the remaining ½ cup (125 mL) of cheese and 1 tablespoon (15 mL) of chives. Cover the dish with foil and top with a small bowl or plate to keep the sandwiches submerged. Refrigerate for at least 6 hours, but overnight is best.
4. Preheat the oven to 350°F (180°C). Bake, covered with buttered foil, for 30 minutes. Remove the foil and bake for another 30 to 35 minutes or until puffed and golden brown (the casserole will deflate as it cools). Serve warm straight from the casserole dish with mustard on the side.

1 cup (250 mL) grated Swiss cheese

1 cup (250 mL) grated white cheddar cheese

6 day-old croissants

2 tablespoons (30 mL) Dijon mustard, plus extra for serving

12 slices deli-style ham

4 teaspoons (20 mL) finely chopped fresh chives, divided

6 large eggs

1¼ cups (310 mL) milk

1 clove garlic, grated or pressed

1½ teaspoons (7 mL) kosher salt

½ teaspoon (2 mL) freshly ground black pepper

OUR FAVOURITE PANCAKES

VEGETARIAN, KID FRIENDLY, QUICK COOKING

Serves 2 to 4

3 tablespoons (45 mL) unsalted butter, plus extra for cooking

1 cup (250 mL) buttermilk

1 large egg

1 teaspoon (5 mL) vanilla bean paste or pure vanilla extract

1 cup (250 mL) all-purpose flour

1 tablespoon (15 mL) granulated sugar

1 tablespoon (15 mL) baking powder

½ teaspoon (2 mL) baking soda

½ teaspoon (2 mL) kosher salt

I've been making these pancakes for my boys for as long as they've been alive, and surprisingly I've yet to share the recipe anywhere. There is nothing particularly special about them—they're made with ordinary ingredients like flour, butter, buttermilk, and eggs—but it's the breakfast recipe my sons request most often. I like to cook my pancakes in butter, but it's really easy to burn, so I use a piece of paper towel to wipe out my skillet after every other batch. Be sure to choose a heavy-bottomed skillet like cast iron for pancakes; if your skillet is too thin, your pancakes are likely to burn.

1. Preheat the oven to 200°F (95°C).
2. Melt the butter in a medium to large cast iron, stainless steel, or non-stick skillet set over medium heat. Meanwhile, in a medium bowl, whisk together the buttermilk, egg, and vanilla. Pour the butter into the milk mixture and gently stir to combine.
3. In a second bowl, stir together the flour, sugar, baking powder, baking soda, and salt. Create a well in the middle of the dry ingredients and, just before you're ready to cook, pour in the milk mixture and lightly stir until just combined (lumps are good!).
4. Ladle ¼ cup (60 mL) batter per pancake into the skillet. Cook until surfaces of the pancakes bubble and a few burst, 1 to 2 minutes. Flip carefully and cook until browned on the under-side, 1 minute more.
5. Transfer the pancakes in a single layer on to a sheet of aluminum foil and place in the preheated oven. Continue with more butter and the remaining batter. Serve with your favourite toppings.

TIP: Here are three pancake mix options. **1.** Mash a ripe banana and stir it into the batter. **2.** Chop toasted nuts (see page 253) and fold them into the batter with ½ cup (125 mL) mini-chocolate chips. This is especially good with the banana-laced batter. **3.** Add ½ cup (125 mL) fresh blueberries to the batter after tossing them with a tablespoon of flour. This will prevent them from sinking to the bottom of the pancake.

OVERNIGHT FRENCH TOAST CASSEROLE

Serves 6 to 8

Casseroles are a proven fan fave, and this one was created specifically with you, the cook, in mind. The work, of which there is very little, can be done the night before the dish is needed, meaning that your morning is guaranteed to run smoother. The technique of soaking bread overnight in an egg custard mixture is not new, but the crowd-pleasing part of this dish is the sugary butter sauce that's smeared over the bread before it bakes. Decadent? No doubt. Easy? Impossibly so. Delicious? Let the empty plates speak for themselves.

1 tablespoon (15 mL) unsalted butter

1 loaf stale French bread (about 1 pound/450 g), cut diagonally in 1-inch (2 cm) thick slices

8 large eggs

1½ cups (375 mL) whole milk

1½ cups (375 mL) half-and-half (10%) cream

2 teaspoons (10 mL) pure vanilla extract

1 teaspoon (5 mL) ground cinnamon, divided

¾ cup (175 mL) butter, melted and warm

¾ cup (175 mL) brown sugar

3 tablespoons (45 mL) liquid honey

¼ teaspoon (1 mL) ground nutmeg

For serving (optional)

Chopped or sliced fresh fruit

Powdered sugar

Chopped nuts

1. Generously butter a 9- × 13-inch (23 × 33 cm) enamel roasting pan and arrange the slices of bread over the bottom, overlapping the pieces if necessary.
2. In a large bowl, beat together eggs, milk, cream, vanilla, and ½ teaspoon (2 mL) cinnamon. Pour over the bread slices, cover, and refrigerate overnight.
3. The next morning, preheat the oven to 350°F (180°C). Remove the casserole from the refrigerator and let it come to room temperature while the oven preheats. Check the dish and assess the amount of liquid remaining. The bread should have absorbed almost all of it, but if it didn't, pour some out; there should be roughly ½ inch (1 cm) of liquid left on the bottom of the dish. (If there is more than that, the bread wasn't dry enough to absorb it all.)
4. In a medium bowl, whisk together the warm melted butter, brown sugar, honey, remaining ½ teaspoon (2 mL) cinnamon, and nutmeg until the sugar is mostly dissolved. Smear the topping over the moist bread and bake, uncovered, for 40 minutes. Serve at once, topped with fresh fruit, powdered sugar, and nuts, if using.

GOLDEN APRICOT GRANOLA

VEGETARIAN, MAKE AHEAD, KID FRIENDLY,
WHOLE GRAIN, GLUTEN-FREE

Approximately 6 cups (1.5 L)

3 cups (750 mL) old-fashioned
    rolled oats

¾ cup (175 mL) chopped walnuts

½ cup (125 mL) sunflower seeds

½ cup (125 mL) pumpkin seeds

½ teaspoon (2 mL) cinnamon

½ teaspoon (2 mL) ground ginger

½ teaspoon (2 mL) salt

½ cup (125 mL) apricot jam

¼ cup (60 mL) neutral-flavoured oil,
    like sunflower, safflower, or canola

2 tablespoons (30 mL) liquid honey

2 tablespoons (30 mL) water

1 teaspoon (5 mL) vanilla bean paste or
    pure vanilla extract

½ cup (125 mL) golden raisins

½ cup (125 mL) dried cranberries

Most commercially made granolas are laden with excess fat and sugar. A homemade version is so simple to make, tastes so much better than its store-bought counterpart, and is worth the small amount of effort it will take. This one combines oats, nuts, seeds, and plenty of dried fruit, and is bound together with a jammy slurry that sweetens the cereal just enough, but not excessively so. I like to eat it with plain yogurt, or a splash of milk, and believe it always benefits from a blanket of fresh berries.

1. Preheat the oven to 325°F (160°C). Line a rimmed sheet pan with parchment paper and set aside.
2. In a medium bowl, combine the oats, walnuts, sunflower seeds, pumpkin seeds, cinnamon, ginger, and salt. In a second bowl, whisk together the apricot jam, oil, honey, water, and vanilla. Drizzle the apricot mixture over the dry ingredients and toss thoroughly to mix.
3. Spread the mixture onto the prepared pan and bake for 30 to 35 minutes, stirring halfway through the baking time, or until golden brown and fragrant. The browner the granola becomes (without burning), the crunchier it will be.
4. Cool on a wire rack. Break up any oversized clumps while the granola is still warm. Stir in the raisins and cranberries. Store the granola in an airtight container on the counter or in the fridge. It will keep for several weeks.

TIP: To make a golden apricot granola parfait cup, combine ⅔ cup (170 mL) plain Greek yogurt, 1 tablespoon (15 mL) maple syrup, and ½ teaspoon (2 mL) vanilla in a small bowl. Layer yogurt and granola in a clean glass jar or cup and top with fresh fruit.

PECAN SANDIE SPELT SCONES

VEGETARIAN, MAKE AHEAD, KID FRIENDLY,
WHOLE GRAIN

Makes 6 scones

The first time I made these scones they literally disappeared within minutes, so I knew I was on to something. I really had no idea what I was creating until I realized the melt-in-your-mouth texture wasn't unlike that of a pecan shortbread cookie, which is how these got their name. Plump, moist, and subtly sweet, the cream in the recipe replaces the usual milk and butter, simplifying the ingredients list and delivering a dish that's also light and airy.

½ cup (125 mL) pecans

1½ cups (375 mL) spelt flour, plus extra for kneading

3 tablespoons (45 mL) packed brown sugar

1½ teaspoons (7 mL) baking powder

¼ teaspoon (1 mL) salt

1 cup (250 mL) heavy (35%) cream, plus extra for brushing

1 teaspoon (5 mL) pure vanilla extract

2 teaspoons (10 mL) coarse sugar

Optional toppings for serving: jam of your choice, butter, clotted cream

1. Preheat the oven to 425°F (220°C) and line a rimmed sheet pan with parchment paper. Scatter pecans on the pan in an even layer and bake for 5 to 6 minutes or until golden and fragrant.

2. Remove the sheet pan from the oven and let cool for 5 minutes. Transfer pecans to the bowl of a food processor fitted with a steel blade. Set aside the sheet pan; you'll use it later to bake the scones. Process nuts until finely ground.

3. Remove 2 teaspoons (10 mL) of the ground pecans and place in a small bowl. Add the flour, sugar, baking powder, and salt to the food processor and pulse to combine.

4. Pour in the cream and vanilla and pulse again, until the dough just barely comes together.

5. Dump the dough onto a lightly floured counter and gather it up into a ball, collecting any dry bits with your hands. Fold it over itself a couple of times and place it on the lined sheet pan, patting it into a 1-inch (2.5 cm) thick circle.

6. Brush the top of the dough round with a bit of cream. Add coarse sugar to the reserved ground pecans and stir to combine. Scatter evenly over the dough and cut into 6 wedges with a sharp knife. Pull the scones apart by at least 2 inches (5 cm) so they have room to brown.

7. Bake for 15 to 18 minutes or until the tops and edges are golden brown and firm. Allow to cool on the sheet pan for 5 minutes before serving with jam, butter, and clotted cream.

SPICED PUMPKIN QUINOA MUFFINS

Makes 12 muffins

¾ cup (175 mL) whole wheat flour

½ cup (125 mL) all-purpose flour

1 teaspoon (5 mL) baking soda

½ teaspoon (2 mL) baking powder

1 teaspoon (5 mL) ground cinnamon

½ teaspoon (2 mL) ground ginger

½ teaspoon (2 mL) kosher salt

½ cup (125 mL) packed brown sugar

¼ cup (60 mL) liquid honey

1 large egg

¼ cup (60 mL) plain Greek yogurt

¼ cup (60 mL) canola, sunflower, or
melted coconut oil

1 teaspoon (5 mL) vanilla bean paste or
pure vanilla extract

¾ cup (175 mL) pure pumpkin purée

½ cup (125 mL) cooked quinoa

On average, the food-inhaling adolescents in my house go through a dozen muffins every day or so. I might have one for breakfast with them, or with my daily cup of afternoon tea, and my husband usually sneaks one when he walks in the door after work, but other than that the boys take care of the whole batch themselves, a feat that still fascinates me. I'm happy to enable their muffin-munching addiction, but there's a catch: the muffins have to do something good for their bodies, not just their taste buds, which is why these are made with whole grains, pumpkin, and quinoa.

1. Preheat the oven to 350°F (180°C). Line a standard muffin tin with 12 paper liners; set aside.
2. In a medium bowl, combine the whole wheat and all-purpose flours, baking soda, baking powder, cinnamon, ginger, and salt. In a large mixing bowl, whisk together the brown sugar, honey, egg, yogurt, oil, and vanilla. Stir in the pumpkin and mix well. Add the dry ingredients and the quinoa to the wet mixture; stir until just combined.
3. Scoop the batter into the prepared muffin tin, filling the cups ⅔ to ¾ full. Bake for 18 to 20 minutes or until the centres are set and the tops are golden brown. Remove from the oven and let cool for 5 minutes before transferring muffins to a cooling rack.

TIP: **1.** Muffins can be made ahead and stored in the freezer, wrapped individually in plastic wrap. To thaw, remove from the freezer and place in the fridge overnight. Warm in the microwave for 30 seconds prior to serving. **2.** I don't specifically cook quinoa for this recipe, but rather I intentionally make extra and store the leftovers in the fridge or freezer so I have it available when the mood—or need—to make muffins strikes. I do the same with the pumpkin as well, measuring it into ¾-cup (175 mL) portions and freezing it in small zip top bags.

ALMOND BUTTER AND JAM
BREAKFAST BARS

VEGETARIAN, MAKE AHEAD,
KID FRIENDLY, WHOLE GRAIN

I love a good crumb bar, and this recipe is the breakfast equivalent. These bars feel decadent, but you can tell from the mostly wholesome ingredients list that they are anything but. I like to serve them to the kids with a smoothie when I'm in a hurry, or on their own as something to take on the go. While I use jam in this recipe (I really love them with the Berry Chia Jam on page 250), sliced or fresh berries scattered over the bottom layer of the bar will work as well. They are easiest to cut once chilled and store exceptionally well in the refrigerator and freezer.

Makes 12 bars

1½ cups (375 mL) old-fashioned rolled oats

½ cup (125 mL) whole wheat flour

½ teaspoon (2 mL) ground cinnamon

¼ teaspoon (1 mL) baking powder

¼ teaspoon (1 mL) kosher salt

½ cup (125 mL) almond butter

½ cup (125 mL) packed light brown sugar

1 large egg

1 teaspoon (5 mL) vanilla bean paste or pure vanilla extract

¾ cup (175 mL) jam, any flavour (I like to use Berry Chia Jam, page 250)

½ cup (125 mL) chopped almonds

1. Preheat the oven to 350°F (180°C). Grease an 8- × 8-inch (20 × 20 cm) baking pan and line with a piece of parchment paper, leaving a 2-inch (5 cm) overhang on two sides.

2. In the bowl of a food processor fitted with a steel blade, make the base by pulsing the oats, flour, cinnamon, baking powder, and salt until finely ground. Add the almond butter, brown sugar, egg, and vanilla and pulse to combine. The mixture should resemble wet sand. If it doesn't, and appears to be too dry, add a tablespoon (15 mL) of water to the mixture. Reserve ½ cup (125 mL) of the crumble mixture and set aside.

3. Press the remaining crumble mixture evenly into the prepared pan. Spread the jam over the bottom crust. Combine chopped almonds and reserved crumble mixture, and scatter over the jam.

4. Bake for 25 to 30 minutes or until the top is golden brown. Cool completely, then remove from pan using the parchment paper overhang. Cut into 12 bars. Bars can be stored in an airtight container for up to 5 days.

DUTCH OVEN 101: THE WONDER POT

This heavy-duty, thick-bottomed pot with a tight-fitting, heatproof lid excels at stewing and braising, making soups and chilis, and cooking grains like rice and quinoa. It can sit on the stovetop or slide into the oven, depending on the type of meal you are making. Sometimes referred to as a casserole, cocotte, or French oven, the terms can be used interchangeably, but there is a slight difference. Dutch oven originally referred to a heavy, black cast iron pot, whereas French oven describes a colourful, enamel-coated cast iron pot, which is likely what you cook with at home. The term *French oven* never really took off in North America, so for consistency's sake these pots are also known as Dutch ovens. Here's one way to think of it: a French oven is a type of Dutch oven, not a different pot altogether. Regardless, nothing in my kitchen gets more of a workout than these hard-working wonder pots.

WHAT TO LOOK FOR

Dutch ovens are available in round and oval shapes; which shape you choose is a matter of personal preference, although round pots do fit better over a stovetop burner. They range from teeny tiny (1 quart/950 mL) to jumbo (13 quarts/12 L), but I tend to keep just two sizes on hand: medium and large. A medium-size pot (4 to 6 quarts/3.8 to 5.7 L) is appropriate for most recipes; it can sear a pork shoulder, roast a chicken, or simmer a pot of soup and is ideal for feeding 2 to 4 people. If you regularly feed more, you may want to invest in a 7- to 9-quart (6.6 to 8.5 L) pot. I have a collection of Dutch ovens made by Le Creuset, Staub, and Lodge—plus a vintage Dansk Kobenstyle—but other brands are equally as capable and often made with the same features: a thick, flat bottom with equally thick vertical sides and an inner lip around the top that provides a closed seal when the lid is placed correctly. What separates top-of-line Dutch ovens from the rest of the pack are the small details, such as handle size (something that shouldn't be underestimated when you're lugging a heavy stew out of the oven), ease of cleaning, and quality of enamel coating (good coatings remain chip-free after years of use). When it comes to actually cooking, most can be used interchangeably. Dutch ovens can be purchased new at specialty kitchen stores or department stores, but you can also look for vintage and used pots online or at your local thrift store or antique market. The cost of a Dutch oven varies greatly depending on the material used to make it, the size of the pot, and the quality of the construction. Basic seasoned cast iron pots can be found for $60 or so, whereas similar-size enamel-coated Dutch ovens can cost hundreds of dollars but are generally worth the investment.

CARING FOR AND CLEANING DUTCH OVENS

Cleaning a Dutch oven properly is vital because you don't want to strip away or chip at the enamel coating. Essentially non-stick, these pots require nothing more than a long soak and a good scrubbing with mild soap and warm water. If you happen to burn something to the bottom of your pot—it's happened to me more times than I care to count—cover the bottom with water, bring to a boil, and sprinkle with baking soda. Let it soak and then scrub with a soft sponge or dishcloth. Whatever you do, do not use steel wool on your pot or the enamel coating will be ruined. Trust me. I speak from experience. For more information on the care of your pot, consult the manufacturer or the store where you purchased it.

HOW TO STORE

There's nothing too complicated about storing a Dutch oven, but I do have one important thought to share: thoroughly dry any Dutch oven before storing it in a dry cupboard, preferably away from steam (i.e., over an oven). If it is put away damp, mould can grow on and around the wet spots in the pot. Again, I speak from experience.

TOP TIPS FOR USE

- Dutch ovens reliably can be used on any stovetop (gas, electric, induction, etc.) and with any oven or grill.

- To protect their surfaces, silicone, rubber, wooden, or heat-resistant plastic tools are recommended for use with enamel-coated Dutch ovens. Metal tools can be used with care—they should not skim the bottom of the pot. If you're making soup or something that needs to be puréed, do not use an immersion blender in the pot, as you can—and likely will—chip the enamel. Instead, transfer the soup to a bowl before blending.

- Dutch ovens can also be used to keep foods cool; chill the pot, fill the bottom with ice, and it quickly transforms into a server for cold food.

SOUPS, STEWS, AND CHILIS

I HAVE COME to believe that anyone who walks into a kitchen should know how to make soup. Very few people are immune to the seductive powers of this classic comfort food, and there is no end to the things you can put in the pot. Meat is nice, and so are vegetables, beans, and noodles. A garnish of grated cheese or, even better, toasted bread can elevate the dish to something special, and the ingredients you choose allow the dish to be tailored to suit almost any season. The same can be said for stews and chilis. I think of this as real soul food; these are soothing dishes, perfect for feeding plenty of people easily and economically. Take my Creamy Beef Stroganoff Soup (page 67), for example; it is satisfyingly simple to make yet worthy of ladling out to guests. The Simple Lentil Soup (page 55) remains one of my boys' favourite meals and is something I make for them when they are sick, sad, or in need of some edible comfort. Like the lentil soup, the Smoky Corn and Cheddar Chowder (page 56), Cream of Mushroom Soup with Mustard and Lemon (page 59), and Potatoes, Greens, and Beans Potage (page 60) can easily be made vegetarian by using vegetable broth in place of chicken broth. And if you're looking for a way to boost the vegetable intake of picky eaters, search no further; among the many options in this chapter, I'd recommend the Chicken and Wild Rice Soup (page 61). Soups, stews, and chilis really are the original one-pot meals!

Makes 10 cups (2.5 L)

1 whole chicken (3 to 4 pounds/1.4 to 1.8 kg), rinsed and giblets discarded
2 small onions, halved
2 carrots, cut in large chunks
2 celery stalks, cut in large chunks
12 cups (3 L) cold water
1 head garlic, halved
½ bunch parsley
2 bay leaves
2 teaspoons (10 mL) peppercorns
Kosher salt

WHOLE CHICKEN BROTH

MAKE AHEAD, KID FRIENDLY, GLUTEN-FREE

I've always been a big fan of cooking once in order to eat two or three times, and this chicken broth is a perfect example of that ideology in practice. Unlike many chicken broth recipes, mine uses a whole raw chicken instead of only the bones. This brings more flavour to the broth and also leaves me with a container full of cooked chicken meat to stir into my Twenty-Minute Chicken Noodle Soup (page 52), stuff into sandwiches and tacos, add to salads, or scatter over pizza.

1. Place the chicken, onions, carrots, and celery in a large Dutch oven (7 to 9 quarts/6.6 to 8.5 L) and set over medium-high heat.
2. Cover with 12 cups (3 L) cold water. Toss in the garlic, parsley, bay leaves, and peppercorns and bring to a boil. Immediately reduce heat to medium-low, and skim any foam from the surface of the water. Partially cover the pot and simmer for 1 to 1½ hours. Allow to cool in the pot for at least 30 minutes.
3. Using tongs, carefully transfer the chicken to a cutting board or large bowl. When cool enough to handle, discard the skin and bones. Shred the meat and store in a covered container in the fridge for future use.
4. Strain the broth through a fine-mesh sieve lined with paper towel or cheesecloth. Discard the vegetables and herbs. Season to taste with salt and use the broth immediately, or let cool before storing in an air-tight container in the refrigerator for 3 to 4 days or in the freezer for up to 6 months.

TIP: Feel free to add any reserved bones you may have (for example, the backbone from the Flat Roasted Chicken with Farro on page 123) to the broth for extra flavour.

HERBED PARMESAN BROTH

VEGETARIAN, MAKE AHEAD,
KID FRIENDLY, GLUTEN-FREE

Makes 5 to 6 cups (1.25 to 1.5 L)

I save my Parmesan cheese rinds and store them in a container in the freezer, making this broth a cinch to make. You might want to become friends with your local deli owner and ask if you can purchase their rinds for a small fee. Most will be happy to sell them to you. If using true Parmesan, the rind shouldn't have a wax coating. If yours happens to, lightly shave it off with a vegetable peeler. To keep the rinds from sticking to the bottom of your pot—and they *will* get gummy and adhere themselves, making a bit of a mess—you can tie them up in a piece of cheesecloth and hang them from a spoon that rests across the top of the pot. That way, the flavour of the cheese will infuse the broth without leaving cheesy bits on the bottom of the pot.

1½ cups (375 mL) chopped Parmesan
　　cheese rind (about 6½ ounces/190 g)
8 cups (2 L) water
4 to 6 thyme sprigs
4 to 6 parsley sprigs
1 small onion, peeled and quartered
3 cloves garlic, peeled and smashed
Kosher salt

1. In a medium Dutch oven (4 to 6 quarts/3.8 to 5.7 L), bring the Parmesan, water, thyme, parsley, onion, and garlic to a boil. Lower the heat to medium-low and simmer for 1 hour.
2. Strain the broth through a fine-mesh sieve lined with paper towel or cheesecloth. Discard the solid matter. Season to taste with salt and use the broth immediately, or let cool before storing in an air-tight container in the refrigerator for 3 to 4 days or in the freezer for up to 6 months.

TIP: If you have a teething baby, a frozen Parmesan cheese rind makes an excellent and soothing teether.

TWENTY-MINUTE
CHICKEN NOODLE SOUP

Serves 4 to 6

8 cups (2 L) Whole Chicken Broth
(page 48) or low-sodium store-
bought chicken broth

3 celery stalks, diced (about 1 cup/
250 mL)

3 medium carrots, diced (about
1 cup/250 mL)

2 cups (500 mL) broad egg noodles

3 cups (750 mL) shredded or chopped
cooked chicken

1 cup (250 mL) frozen peas

¼ cup (60 mL) chopped fresh parsley

Kosher salt

Freshly ground black pepper

This may be the easiest chicken noodle soup you'll ever make, but there is one caveat to consider before you begin making it: use the very best chicken broth available (I use my Whole Chicken Broth on page 48) because it will affect the overall taste of the dish. It's impossible to stress how true this is and the impact a subpar broth can have on the end result. Also, don't forget to season the soup at the end. I haven't suggested an amount for this because I think you should decide for yourself based on the broth you use. My kids are crazy for this soup, and for reasons I can't quite understand, it's the only way I can get my toddler to consume his carrots.

1. In a medium Dutch oven (4 to 6 quarts/3.8 to 5.7 L), bring the chicken broth to a simmer over medium-high heat. Add the celery and carrots, and simmer uncovered for 10 minutes. Add the noodles and cooked chicken and cook for another 7 to 10 minutes or just until the noodles and vegetables are tender.

2. Stir in the peas and parsley and cook for another minute or two or until the peas are heated through. Season with salt and pepper to taste. Ladle into bowls and serve at once.

SIMPLE LENTIL SOUP

Serves 4 to 6

As the title implies, this lentil soup couldn't be simpler to make, yet to this day it remains beloved by my boys and is one of the meals they request most often. Hearty and economical, it is great served for either lunch or dinner. The flavour improves if you make it a day or so in advance, so consider simmering a pot on Sunday for an already-made meatless Monday meal, or for a week's worth of workday or school lunches.

1. In a medium Dutch oven (4 to 6 quarts/3.8 to 5.7 L), heat the oil over medium-high heat. Add the onions, carrots, celery, garlic, and a generous pinch of salt. Sauté until vegetables are slightly golden, about 5 minutes.
2. Add the pepper, cumin, and tomato paste, and cook for another 1 to 2 minutes, stirring constantly. Make sure the vegetables are evenly coated in the tomato paste and spice mixture.
3. Add the lentils, bay leaf, thyme, broth, and another pinch of salt. Bring to a boil, skimming off any foam that rises to the surface. Reduce the heat and simmer for 45 to 60 minutes or until the lentils are tender but still hold their shape.
4. Stir in the tamari and season to taste with additional salt and pepper, if needed. Ladle into bowls and serve topped with sour cream or yogurt, if using.

TIP: I find this soup tastes best a day or so after it's made, so I'd suggest making a batch on the weekend and serving it for dinner early in the week.

2 tablespoons (30 mL) olive oil

1 small onion, chopped (about ½ cup/125 mL)

2 medium carrots, peeled and chopped (about ¾ cup/175 mL)

2 celery stalks, chopped (about ¾ cup/175 mL)

2 cloves garlic, grated or pressed

Kosher salt

½ teaspoon (2 mL) freshly ground black pepper

1 teaspoon (5 mL) ground cumin

1 tablespoon (15 mL) tomato paste

2 cups (500 mL) brown or green lentils, rinsed

1 bay leaf

1 sprig fresh thyme, leaves removed

8 cups (2 L) Whole Chicken Broth (page 48) or low-sodium store-bought chicken broth

1 tablespoon (15 mL) tamari or soy sauce

Sour cream or plain yogurt, for garnish (optional)

SMOKY CORN AND CHEDDAR CHOWDER

Serves 4 to 6

1 tablespoon (15 mL) butter

1 tablespoon (15 mL) olive oil

1 large Spanish onion, diced (about
   1½ cups/375 mL)

Kosher salt

1 pound (450 g) new potatoes,
   unpeeled and diced

3 cups (750 mL) Whole Chicken Broth
   (page 48) or low-sodium store-
   bought chicken broth

6 sprigs fresh thyme

4 cups (1 L) fresh corn (from about 6 to
   7 ears) or frozen corn (thawed)

4 green onions, trimmed and thinly
   sliced, divided

1 cup (250 mL) milk

⅓ cup (85 mL) heavy (35%) cream

1 teaspoon (5 mL) ground cumin

1 teaspoon (5 mL) smoked paprika

½ teaspoon (2 mL) freshly ground
   black pepper

1 cup (250 mL) grated extra-old sharp
   cheddar cheese

Chopped fresh basil or dill sprigs, for
   garnish

How do you feel about eating soup in the summer? I love it, but have to confess I'm not a fan of cold soups. To me, eating them is like downing a vegetable smoothie with a spoon, and I just can't get behind the idea. What I like best about this dish is that it's made with a handful of basic foods you're likely to have on hand and it's infused with just enough spice to remind us that fall really is right around the corner. The simple simmer of a few ingredients makes this a dinner that can be pulled together quickly (no lengthy stovetop time required) using the best of the season in a fresh and fun way.

1. In a medium Dutch oven (4 to 6 quarts/3.8 to 5.7 L), heat the butter and oil over medium-high heat. Add the onion, sprinkle with a generous pinch of salt, and sauté until the onion is translucent and slightly browned, 4 to 5 minutes. Add the potatoes to the pot along with the broth, thyme, and another pinch of salt. Bring to a boil, reduce heat, and simmer for 10 to 15 minutes or until the potatoes are tender and can be pierced with a fork.

2. Add the corn, all but 2 tablespoons (30 mL) of the green onions, milk, and cream to the pot. Bring to a boil, reduce heat slightly, and allow to bubble for 7 to 8 minutes. Stir in the cumin, paprika, and pepper. Discard the thyme. Take the pot off the heat and stir in the cheese, allowing it to melt completely. Ladle into bowls and serve at once garnished with remaining green onions and basil or dill.

CREAM OF MUSHROOM SOUP WITH MUSTARD AND LEMON

Serves 4

Although you can use any kind of mushroom in this soup, I tend to stick to cremini, a more mature version of the classic white button mushroom. I find its darker colour more appealing and its flavour more complex than that of its younger cousin. To clean mushrooms, I brush them off with a dampened paper towel, but if they're excessively dirty I will run them under cool water before patting them dry. Like most soups, this one tastes better the longer it hangs out in the refrigerator, so don't hesitate to make it a day or two in advance if possible.

2 tablespoons (30 mL) olive oil

4 tablespoons (60 mL) butter, divided

1 small onion, finely chopped

Kosher salt

2 cloves garlic, grated or pressed

1½ pounds (675 g) cremini mushrooms, roughly chopped or thinly sliced (about 6 cups/1.5 L)

2 sprigs fresh thyme, leaves stripped

Freshly ground black pepper

¼ cup (60 mL) all-purpose flour

4 cups (1 L) Whole Chicken Broth (page 48) or low-sodium store-bought chicken broth

½ cup (125 mL) heavy (35%) cream

1 tablespoon (15 mL) Dijon mustard

1½ tablespoons (22 mL) fresh lemon juice (about ½ lemon)

Fresh chives, for garnish

1. In a medium Dutch oven (4 to 6 quarts/3.8 to 5.7 L), heat the oil and 2 tablespoons (30 mL) butter over medium-high heat. Add the onion, sprinkle with a generous pinch of salt, and cook until soft, 2 to 3 minutes. Add the garlic and cook for 1 minute more.

2. Add the mushrooms, thyme, and the remaining 2 tablespoons (30 mL) butter to the pot. Cook until the mushrooms are soft, their moisture cooks off, and they start to turn golden, 10 to 12 minutes. Season with another pinch of salt and freshly ground black pepper.

3. Sprinkle the flour over the vegetables and stir to coat evenly. Cook for 1 to 2 minutes, stirring constantly, to remove the floury taste. There will be some brown bits on the bottom of the pan, but this is a good thing; it will translate to extra flavour in the soup.

4. Add the broth and bring to a boil, scraping up the browned bits on the bottom of the pot. Reduce the heat slightly. When the soup has thickened slightly, about 10 minutes or so, stir in the cream, Dijon, and lemon juice. Check seasonings and add more salt and pepper if needed. Ladle into bowls and garnish with chives.

POTATOES, GREENS, AND BEANS POTAGE

Serves 4 to 6

MAKE AHEAD, KID FRIENDLY

¼ cup (60 mL) olive oil

1 large red onion, small dice (about 1 cup/250 mL)

2 cloves garlic, thinly sliced

Kosher salt

Freshly ground black pepper

2 medium carrots, peeled and cut into ¼-inch (0.5 cm) thick half moons (about 1 cup/250 mL)

3 celery stalks, diced (about 1 cup/ 250 mL)

2 large russet potatoes, scrubbed and diced (about 4 cups/1 L)

¼ cup (60 mL) tomato paste

3 cans (19 ounces/540 mL each) cannellini (white kidney) beans, drained and rinsed

6 cups (1.5 L) Whole Chicken Broth (page 48) or low-sodium store-bought chicken or vegetable broth

1 medium bunch curly kale, stems removed and sliced into ½-inch (1 cm) ribbons (about 8 cups/2 L)

Toasted bread, for serving

Parmesan cheese, for serving

This is my take on ribollita, a hearty Tuscan soup with peasant origins. Often made with bread, beans, and greens, but my version replaces the bread with potatoes, preferring to serve bread on the side instead. If you have any leftover soup, it will thicken in the fridge and lose its soupy consistency. You can thin it out with a little water or broth, or alternatively you can fry the thick mixture in an oil-slicked skillet, just like a potato pancake, and top it with a fried egg for a different meal on another day.

1. In a large Dutch oven (7 to 9 quarts/6.6 to 8.5 L), heat the oil over medium heat. Add the onion, garlic, and a good pinch each of salt and pepper. Cook until the onion is soft and translucent, 3 to 5 minutes.

2. Add the carrots, celery, and potatoes to the pot and cook for another 5 minutes, stirring occasionally. Add the tomato paste and cook for 1 minute more, stirring constantly. Tip in the beans and broth and bring to a boil.

3. Lower the heat and simmer, uncovered, for 1 to 1½ hours or until the soup has thickened and the vegetables are soft. Stir in the kale and simmer until tender and wilted, 5 to 8 minutes. Check seasonings and add more salt and pepper if needed. Ladle into bowls and serve at once with toasted bread and Parmesan cheese.

CHICKEN AND WILD RICE SOUP

MAKE AHEAD, KID FRIENDLY, WHOLE GRAIN,
GLUTEN-FREE

Serves 4 to 6

This soup is warm and cozy, and utterly essential for the fall and winter seasons. It's also a tried and true family favourite, beloved by all from the toddler to the septuagenarians who join us for Sunday supper. It's quick to prepare, nourishing, and so comforting you'll want to eat it all winter long. I make it a lot in December, when the calendar is full of social events, shopping, gift-wrapping, work, school concerts, cooking, and baking, and the people I live with still seem to require three meals a day to survive. This is the dinner that saves me. (Sadly, humans cannot live off Toblerone alone!) In the weeks following Thanksgiving and Christmas, your leftover turkey will make a nice substitute for the chicken in this recipe.

2 tablespoons (30 mL) coconut oil

3 large carrots, diced (about 1 cup/ 250 mL)

3 celery stalks, diced (about 1 cup/ 250 mL)

1 medium onion, diced (about 1 cup/ 250 mL)

1 cup (250 mL) chopped baby bok choy

Kosher salt

1½ cups (375 mL) wild rice (or use brown rice, basmati rice, or a combination)

1 teaspoon (5 mL) curry powder

1 teaspoon (5 mL) cumin

8 cups (2 L) Whole Chicken Broth (page 48) or low-sodium store-bought chicken broth

2 cups (500 mL) diced boneless, skin-less chicken breasts or thighs (or a mixture of both)

1 can (14 ounces/400 mL) full-fat coconut milk

Freshly ground black pepper (optional)

1. In a medium Dutch oven (4 to 6 quarts/3.8 to 5.7 mL), warm the oil over medium heat and then add the carrots, celery, onions, and bok choy. Season with a generous pinch of salt and cook, stirring frequently, until the vegetables are soft, translucent, and slightly browned.

2. Stir in the rice and sprinkle with the curry powder and cumin. Toss to coat the rice and vegetables in the spices; cook for 1 minute more.

3. Pour in the broth. Bring the soup to a boil and then reduce the heat to a simmer. Add the chicken and coconut milk, stir, and cook for 1 to 2 hours or until the rice is tender (basmati rice will cook much faster than wild rice) and the chicken is cooked through. The liquid will thicken. Season with additional salt and pepper, if using. Ladle into bowls and serve at once.

CALDO VERDE

MAKE AHEAD, KID FRIENDLY, QUICK COOKING, GLUTEN-FREE

Serves 4 to 6

This Portuguese potato and greens soup is one I feed to my family when they fall sick and are bundled up in blankets, all sniffly and sneezing. The red pepper flakes give it a little kick to help clear the sinuses, and the kale and potato are nourishing and healing—or at least my boys believe them to be. More often than not, I use regular or turkey kielbasa in this soup, but their spicier cousin chorizo works just as well and is a more authentic addition to the dish.

1. In a medium Dutch oven (4 to 6 quarts/3.8 to 5.7 L), heat the oil and butter over medium heat. Add the onion, season with a generous pinch of salt, and cook, stirring frequently, until softened, about 5 minutes. Add the garlic and red pepper flakes and cook for another 30 seconds.
2. Add the sausage to the pot and cook, stirring frequently, until browned, about 5 minutes. Pour in the chicken broth and bring to a boil.
3. Add the potatoes and kale and stir. Lower the heat to medium-low, partially cover the pot, and simmer for 30 to 40 minutes or until the potatoes and kale are tender and the soup has a creamy consistency. Season with salt and pepper to taste. Ladle into bowls and serve at once.

1 tablespoon (15 mL) olive oil
1 tablespoon (15 mL) butter
1 medium onion, finely chopped
Kosher salt
4 cloves garlic, grated or pressed
½ teaspoon (2 mL) crushed red pepper flakes
10 ounces (300 g) chorizo or kielbasa sausage, cut into ½-inch (1 cm) thick pieces
4 cups (1 L) Whole Chicken Broth (page 48) or low-sodium store-bought chicken broth
2 medium russet potatoes, peeled and grated (about 3 cups/750 mL)
1 bunch curly kale, centre stem removed and cut into thin ribbons (about 4 cups/1 L, loosely packed)
Freshly ground black pepper

SPRING ITALIAN WEDDING SOUP

Serves 4 to 6

1 pound (450 g) ground chicken

6 tablespoons (90 mL) panko bread
crumbs

2 tablespoons (30 mL) basil pesto
(store-bought or homemade)

2 tablespoons (30 mL) grated
Parmesan cheese

2 cloves garlic, grated or pressed

¼ teaspoon (1 mL) crushed red pepper
flakes

Kosher salt

1 large egg

2 to 3 tablespoons (30 to 45 mL)
olive oil

2 leeks, ends and dark green tops
removed, halved and thinly sliced

2 medium carrots, cut into ¼-inch
(0.5 cm) thick half moons

2 celery stalks, diced

6 cups (1.5 L) Whole Chicken Broth
(page 48) or low-sodium store-
bought chicken broth

¾ cup (175 mL) alphabet pasta

2 tablespoons (30 mL) chopped
fresh dill

5 ounces (140 g) baby spinach leaves

Shaved Parmesan cheese, for garnish

Chopped fresh basil, for serving

Lemon wedges, for serving

Wedding soup often consists of meat and greens, and this light-ened-up version follows suit. It's studded with little meatballs made with chicken, Parmesan, and pesto, plus popular spring vegetables like leeks and spinach. I like to use alphabet pasta to entice my toddler to the table, but orzo or any other petite pasta shape would work just as well.

1. In a medium bowl, combine the ground chicken, panko, pesto, Parmesan, garlic, red pepper flakes, a pinch of salt, and egg. Divide the mixture into 24 meatballs (I like to use a 1-inch/2.5 cm ice cream scoop for this job).

2. In a medium Dutch oven (4 to 6 quarts/3.8 to 5.7 L), heat 2 table-spoons (30 mL) oil over medium heat. Add the meatballs and cook, in batches if necessary, until well browned, about 2 min-utes per side. Transfer to a plate lined with paper towel and set aside.

3. Using the remaining 1 tablespoon (15 mL) oil if necessary, add leeks, carrots, and celery. Season with salt and sauté until slightly softened, about 5 minutes.

4. Cover with the broth and bring to a boil. Add the pasta and meat-balls and reduce heat to a simmer, cooking for 10 minutes or until the pasta is tender.

5. Add the dill and spinach and stir. Cook until the spinach is wilted, about 2 minutes. Check seasonings and adjust if needed. Ladle into bowls and garnish with Parmesan cheese, fresh basil, and lemon wedges.

TIP: See Baked Risotto with Chicken, Leeks, and Lemon on page 120 for how to clean leeks.

CREAMY BEEF STROGANOFF SOUP

KID FRIENDLY, QUICK COOKING

Serves 4 to 6

All the rich and beloved flavours of beef stroganoff are transformed into a quick-cooking one-pot soup thanks to the use of ground beef instead of steak or stewing beef. While I love mushrooms in a classic beef stroganoff, it turns out they aren't an authentic component, having been added only to the most North Americanized versions of the dish. I include mushrooms because I love them, but if they aren't to your liking, you can replace them with extra meat. A word of caution: you'll want to serve this as quickly as possible, as the longer it sits, the more the noodles will soak up the broth. You can, of course, add extra broth to return any leftovers to their original soupy consistency.

1. In a medium Dutch oven (4 to 6 quarts/3.8 to 5.7 L), heat the oil and butter over medium-high heat. Sauté the carrots, onion, and garlic with a generous pinch of salt until the onion is softened, about 2 minutes. Add the beef and mushrooms to the pot. Cook, stirring and breaking up the beef with a potato masher or wooden spoon, until the beef is browned, about 3 minutes.

2. Stir in the mustard, Worcestershire sauce, and tomato paste. Cook for 1 minute more. Add the broth, noodles, and pepper. Boil gently, uncovered, for 5 to 7 minutes or until noodles are tender.

3. In a medium bowl, whisk together the sour cream and flour. Whisk 1 cup (250 mL) of the soup broth into the sour cream mixture until smooth. Add the sour cream mixture to the soup. Cook, stirring constantly, until thickened and bubbly. Add the peas, stir, and cook 1 minute more. Taste and adjust seasonings, if needed. Ladle the hot soup into bowls and top with parsley and, if desired, additional sour cream.

1 tablespoon (15 mL) olive oil

1 tablespoon (15 mL) butter

2 medium carrots, diced (about 1 cup/250 mL)

1 medium onion, diced (about 1 cup/250 mL)

2 cloves garlic, grated or pressed

Kosher salt

1 pound (450 g) ground beef

½ pound (225 g) cremini mushrooms, cut into ¼-inch (0.5 cm) thick slices

1 tablespoon (15 mL) Dijon mustard

1 tablespoon (15 mL) Worcestershire sauce

1 tablespoon (15 mL) tomato paste

4 cups (1 L) beef broth

1½ cups (375 mL) dried egg noodles

¼ teaspoon (1 mL) freshly ground black pepper

½ cup (125 mL) sour cream, plus extra for serving

2 tablespoons (30 mL) all-purpose flour

1 cup (250 mL) frozen peas

Chopped fresh parsley, for garnish

CURRIED CHICKPEAS WITH COCONUT RICE

VEGETARIAN, MAKE AHEAD, KID FRIENDLY,
QUICK COOKING, GLUTEN-FREE

Serves 4 to 6

5 cloves garlic, peeled

3-inch (7.5 cm) piece fresh ginger
(about 1 ounce/30 g), peeled

1 medium yellow onion, peeled and
quartered

2 tablespoons (30 mL) olive oil

4 teaspoons (20 mL) curry powder

¼ teaspoon (1 mL) cayenne pepper

2 teaspoons (10 mL) kosher salt

2 tablespoons (30 mL) tomato paste

2 cans (19 ounces/540 mL each)
chickpeas, drained and rinsed

2 cups (500 mL) basmati rice

1 can (14 ounces/400 mL) full-fat
coconut milk

2¼ cups (560 mL) water or vegetable
broth

Chopped fresh cilantro leaves, for
garnish (optional)

Lime wedges, for serving (optional)

Setting up your mise en place (see page 7) really helps this meal come together, as you have to work quickly to get the aromatics sautéed and seasoned before adding the rice and chickpeas. Once everything is in the pot, you can sit back and relax for thirty minutes or so, or you can use that time to prepare a simple salad to serve on the side. If you decide to use broth instead of water, reduce the salt by about ½ teaspoon (2 mL), depending on the salinity of the broth you use.

1. In a mini food processor or blender, combine garlic, ginger, and onion and pulse until it forms a chunky paste.

2. In a medium Dutch oven (4 to 6 quarts/3.8 to 5.7 L), heat the oil over medium-high heat. Tip in the onion mixture and cook for 2 minutes, stirring frequently. Add the curry powder, cayenne, salt, and tomato paste and cook for another 2 to 3 minutes, stirring constantly.

3. Add the chickpeas and rice to the pot and stir with a wooden spoon, thoroughly coating with the onion mixture. Pour in the coconut milk and water. Stir to combine and bring to a boil.

4. Reduce the heat to medium-low, partially cover, and cook until the rice is tender and the liquid is absorbed, 23 to 25 minutes. Remove from the heat, cover the pot, and let sit for 10 minutes. Spoon into bowls, sprinkle with cilantro, if using, and serve hot with lime wedges on the side, if desired.

VARIATION: Stir ½ cup (125 mL) raisins into the finished dish. Sprinkle with sliced almonds and green onions instead of cilantro, before serving.

PORK AND GREEN SALSA CHILI

MAKE AHEAD, KID FRIENDLY, GLUTEN-FREE

Serves 6

This is one of my go-to cold weather dinners. It's perfect for those dark winter nights when you're chilled to the bone; the scent of the simmering pork and salsa permeates the entire house with warmth. It's also ideal for serving to last-minute or unexpected guests, mostly because it's gluten-free and dairy-free, meaning it will work for anyone who isn't vegan or vegetarian. It's a dish you can bring to a friend who just had a baby, but you might want to include a bag of nacho chips, a jar of salsa, some shredded cheese, and an avocado; adding a beer or two wouldn't hurt either. I would be remiss if I failed to mention that this is also a pretty perfect party dish. Serve alongside a pot of Barbecue Chicken Chili with Cornbread Dumplings (page 72) and a counter full of toppings and no one will be disappointed.

1 to 2 tablespoons (15 to 30 mL) olive oil
1½ pounds (675 g) boneless pork butt, cut into bite-size pieces
Kosher salt
½ teaspoon (2 mL) freshly ground black pepper
1 teaspoon (5 mL) ground cumin
1 jar (15 ounces/430 mL) green salsa
3 cans (19 ounces/540 mL each) cannellini (white kidney) beans, drained and rinsed
2 cups (500 mL) Whole Chicken Broth (page 48) or low-sodium store-bought chicken broth
Optional toppings for serving: chopped fresh cilantro, lime wedges, sliced avocado, shredded cheese, tortilla chips, sour cream, salsa

1. In a medium Dutch oven (4 to 6 quarts/3.8 to 5.7 L), heat the oil over medium heat. Add some of the pork pieces—take care not to crowd the pan—and cook until browned on one side, about 2 to 3 minutes. Turn the pieces over and cook the other side for the same amount of time or until completely browned. Transfer the meat to a plate and repeat with the remaining pork, adding more oil to the pot if necessary.

2. Once all the pork has been browned, return it to the pot with any accumulated juices. Season generously with salt, pepper, and cumin and stir well. Cook for 1 minute more. Add the salsa, beans, and broth. Bring to a boil, then reduce heat to a simmer.

3. Cook, uncovered, for 2 to 2½ hours, stirring occasionally, or until the liquid thickens and resembles gravy. Check seasonings and adjust if needed. Ladle into bowls and garnish with your favourite optional toppings.

BARBECUE CHICKEN CHILI WITH CORNBREAD DUMPLINGS

Serves 6 to 8

Adding cheddar and cilantro to this dish makes it a little extra splashy. Chicken replaces the traditional beef often found in chili, and barbecue sauce boosts the overall flavour.

For the chili

3 tablespoons (45 mL) olive oil, divided

2½ pounds (1.1 kg) boneless, skinless chicken thighs or breasts

1 cup (250 mL) diced red onion

1 jalapeño pepper, seeded and diced

3 cloves garlic, grated or pressed

1½ tablespoons (22 mL) smoked paprika

2 tablespoons (30 mL) chili powder

1 tablespoon (15 mL) ground cumin

1 teaspoon (5 mL) kosher salt

½ teaspoon (2 mL) cayenne pepper

2 cans (19 ounces/540 mL each) black beans, drained and rinsed

2 cups (500 mL) frozen corn kernels

1 cup (250 mL) Whole Chicken Broth (page 48) or low-sodium store-bought chicken broth

1 can (28 ounces/796 mL) crushed tomatoes

½ cup (125 mL) barbecue sauce

For the dumplings

1 cup (250 mL) all-purpose flour

1 cup (250 mL) medium-grind cornmeal

2 tablespoons (30 mL) light brown sugar

2 teaspoons (10 mL) baking powder

½ teaspoon (2 mL) kosher salt

3 tablespoons (45 mL) unsalted butter, melted

2 large eggs, beaten

½ cup (125 mL) milk

1 cup (250 mL) shredded cheddar cheese

¼ cup (60 mL) chopped fresh cilantro

For serving (optional)

Sour cream

Sliced green onions

Lime wedges

1. Preheat the oven to 325°F (160°C). In a large Dutch oven (7 to 9 quarts/6.6 to 8.5 L), heat a tablespoon (15 mL) or so of oil over medium-high heat. When the oil is shimmering, add the chicken, cooking until browned on one side. Flip the chicken over and brown the other side. Work in batches if necessary, transferring chicken to a plate and adding more oil as needed, so as not to overcrowd your pot. Don't worry if some of the chicken sticks to the bottom of the pot. It will release when the liquid is added.

2. Stir in the onion, jalapeño, and garlic and cook until they begin to soften, 3 to 5 minutes. Return the chicken to the pot and sprinkle in the smoked paprika, chili powder, cumin, salt, and cayenne. Stir and cook for another 1 to 2 minutes or until the chicken and onions are coated evenly and the spices are fragrant.

3. Add the beans, corn, broth, tomatoes, and barbecue sauce. Bring to a boil, stir, cover, and transfer to the preheated oven. Bake for 2 hours, remove the lid from the pot, and bake for an additional 30 to 60 minutes or until the chicken is tender and the liquid has partially reduced.

4. Remove the chili from the oven and, using 2 forks, shred the chicken inside the pot. Check seasonings and adjust, adding more salt and pepper, if needed.

5. To make the dumplings, increase the oven heat to 400°F (200°C). In a medium mixing bowl, whisk together the flour, cornmeal, brown sugar, baking powder, and salt. Make a well in the centre of the dry ingredients and add the melted butter, eggs, and milk. Stir until just combined, being careful not to overmix. Fold in the cheddar cheese and cilantro.

6. Gently drop large dollops of the batter onto the chili. Bake, uncovered, for 18 to 20 minutes or until the dumplings are cooked through and golden brown. Serve hot with sour cream, green onions, and lime wedges, if using.

TIP: You can make the chili up to 3 days in advance, if desired. Follow the recipe through step 4, then tuck the pot in the refrigerator until needed. Let the chili come to room temperature and then reheat at 325°F (160°C) for 20 minutes before proceeding with the remainder of the recipe.

OVEN-BAKED BALSAMIC BEEF AND VEGETABLE STEW

Serves 4 to 6

Baking unattended for hours, this oven-cooked version of an old-fashioned beef stew is sure to help you win the hearts of your friends and family. Small chunks of beef crisp up in the oven before settling in for a long swim in a bath of balsamic vinegar and beef broth. If you don't like the flavour of balsamic vinegar, you can easily swap it for red wine; just be sure to use a variety you also enjoy drinking so you can serve a glass or two alongside the stew.

1. Preheat the oven to 450°F (230°C).
2. In a medium bowl, stir together the flour, paprika, salt, and pepper. Add the beef and toss to combine, ensuring the beef is evenly coated in the flour.
3. Drizzle the oil into a 9- × 13-inch (23 × 33 cm) casserole dish. Add the meat and toss to coat in the oil. Bake for 12 to 15 minutes or until the beef begins to brown. Remove the dish from the oven and decrease heat to 300°F (150°C).
4. Add the potatoes, carrots, onion, and celery to the beef and stir well. In a small bowl or glass measuring cup, whisk together the beef broth, balsamic vinegar, tomato paste, and sugar. Pour the liquid over the beef and vegetables and shake the pan back and forth a few times to evenly distribute. Add the bay leaves and cover the dish with aluminum foil.
5. Bake for 2½ hours, then uncover and bake for another 30 to 60 minutes or until the meat is tender and the sauce has thickened. Add the peas and stir, cooking until warmed through, about 2 minutes. Spoon into bowls and garnish with parsley.

3 tablespoons (45 mL) all-purpose flour

1 teaspoon (5 mL) paprika

½ teaspoon (2 mL) kosher salt

½ teaspoon (2 mL) freshly ground black pepper

1½ pounds (675 g) stewing beef, cut into 1-inch (2.5 cm) cubes

2 tablespoons (30 mL) olive oil

2 cups (500 mL) chopped Yukon Gold or russet potatoes

4 medium carrots, diced (about 2 cups/500 mL)

1 medium onion, diced (about 1 cup/250 mL)

3 celery stalks, diced (about 1 cup/ 125 mL)

2 cans (10 ounces/284 mL each) condensed beef broth

½ cup (125 mL) balsamic vinegar

2 tablespoons (30 mL) tomato paste

1 teaspoon (5 mL) granulated sugar

2 bay leaves

1 cup (250 mL) frozen peas, thawed

Chopped fresh parsley, for garnish

SHEET PAN 101: THE KITCHEN WORKHORSE

Often referred to as cookie sheets or baking pans, sheet pans are shallow-rimmed, rectangular metal pans available in either a shiny or a dull, dark finish. They can be called on for any number of cooking tasks, including roasting vegetables, cooking meats, making granola, or baking cookies, to name a few. The low sides allow for easy browning and promote even heat circulation. Be careful not to confuse this type of pan with a rimless cookie sheet, which makes quick work of removing delicate baked goods off the surface thanks to its flat sides but won't be able to do double duty as a roasting pan for vegetables and meats.

WHAT TO LOOK FOR

Sheet pans are available in several sizes, but the standard large pan, usually referred to as a half-sheet pan, measures 13 × 18 inches (33 × 45 cm), which is big enough to cook a dinner for four people. Most standard ovens are fitted with baking racks that are roughly 22 inches (55 cm) wide, so this size of pan is perfect because it gives the heat room to circulate. You can also purchase a two-thirds sheet pan (also called a three-quarters sheet pan), which measures 15 × 21 inches (38 × 53 cm), for larger quantities of food. Full sheet pans are 18 × 26 inches (45 × 65 cm) and are usually too large to fit in a home oven. Quarter-sheet pans measure 10 × 15 inches (25 × 38 cm) and are ideal for toasting nuts (page 253) or baking a small batch of cookies. Sheet pans with non-stick coatings are readily available, but I tend to steer clear of those because they are more prone to warping and uneven cooking, not to mention harsh chemical coatings that may leach into food when heated to high temperatures. Another downside to non-stick pans is that they eventually will need to be replaced, as the coating does wear off over time. My personal preference is aluminum pans, which tend to be thicker, heavier, and more durable, are less likely to warp, and heat up more evenly than those made of other materials. Darker pans tend to cook and brown food more quickly than lighter pans, so take that into account when cooking with

them. Sheet pans are readily available at restaurant supply and specialty food stores, and sometimes even at department or warehouse stores, and most can be purchased for under $20.

CARING FOR AND CLEANING SHEET PANS

Of all the sheet pans I own (and I have six—but then again, I wrote a book about them), the one I like best is well loved, very well used, and sports a patina of baked-on oil that I like to think of as "seasoning." It's easily the hardest-working one of the bunch, and I find myself reaching for it time and time again because I like the way it looks. All of this is to say: don't make yourself crazy trying to restore your sheet pans to their original shiny state, because the well-worn ones work just as well. However, there are a few things you can do to keep your pans sparkling if you cringe at the sight of that dark discoloration. For starters, if you line a sheet pan with parchment paper or aluminum foil, finished foods can be removed easily with minimal mess left behind. Simply clean your pan with mild detergent and warm water to remove any residue that lingers. If you skip lining the pan, sometimes there will be stains that just won't come clean with soap and water, and you'll need to turn to a more aggressive cleaning solution. For this, fill a sink with hot water and add equal parts baking soda and vinegar (about ⅓ cup/85 mL each). Soak the pan in the solution for 30 to 60 minutes, rotating it halfway through the soaking time. Then, scrub away the debris with a scouring pad, scrub brush, or steel wool. Wash the pan again with mild detergent and hot water and pat dry to prevent rusting.

HOW TO STORE

If sheet pans are washed and dried, they can be stacked and stored anywhere. For people with limited cabinet space, a tall upright basket is a great option, especially if you own an oversize pan. Cabinets with dividers are another great option, as is the bottom drawer of an oven. For those with space constraints (like me), storing them in the oven works well, too. Just don't forget to remove them before you turn it on.

TOP TIPS FOR USE

- Sheet pans can be used for so much more than baking cookies and roasting dinner. Use them for freezing individual foods like berries, cherries, and other fruits you plan to store in the freezer, or for reheating convenience foods such as frozen pot pies and chicken nuggets.
- When setting up your mise en place (see page 7), instead of using small bowls and dirtying a lot of dishes, cut down on the washing by organizing chopped ingredients in piles on a sheet pan.

BREADS, SANDWICHES, AND PIZZAS

IT'S HARD TO overstate the importance of bread in many cultures. The French are famous for their daily baguettes, in India chapati is served regularly with curries and lentil soup, and according to the Guinness World Records, the Turkish boast the largest per capita consumption of bread in the world. Typically, baking bread is a very time-consuming task and you have to treat it like a small child, giving it plenty of care and attention. My goal with this chapter is to provide easy bread recipes that won't intimidate and that can be prepared from start to finish in a single vessel. From my Jalapeño Popper Rolls (page 91) made in a springform pan, to Honey, Thyme, and Cheddar Skillet Cornbread (page 83) whipped up in a skillet, to Overnight Faux Sourdough (page 80) baking in a Dutch oven, using one pot or pan naturally simplifies the process and provides a launching point for your bread baking adventures. Sandwiches and pizzas round out this section, because it's nearly impossible to find someone who doesn't crave the comforts of this food group.

Serves 4 to 6; makes 1 round boule

VEGETARIAN, MAKE AHEAD, KID FRIENDLY

3 cups (750 mL) all-purpose flour

1½ teaspoons (7 mL) kosher salt

¾ teaspoon (4 mL) instant dry yeast

1 cup (250 mL) warm water

½ cup (125 mL) 2% or full-fat Greek
    yogurt

1 teaspoon (5 mL) liquid honey

A few years ago, I stumbled on a pizza dough recipe that called for nothing more than self-rising flour and Greek yogurt. Doubtful that it would work, I made four pizzas in three days just to prove to myself that this interesting ingredient combination really could deliver a crust worthy of our weekly pizzas. It did indeed succeed, but my kids weren't crazy about the slight tang they detected in the dough. I continued to experiment and came up with a no-knead Dutch oven bread, only this time the tang was welcomed, as it was reminiscent of our favourite sourdough bread I often bought from a local bakery. I usually mix up the dough after dinner and let it rise on the counter while I tend to other tasks. Then, I slip the bowl into the refrigerator overnight and bake the bread the following morning.

1. In the bowl of a stand mixer, combine the flour, salt, yeast, water, yogurt, and honey. Using the paddle attachment, mix until the flour is completely incorporated. Alternatively, you can mix the dough with a wooden spoon until it comes together. The dough will be wet and sticky. Cover the bowl with plastic wrap and let it sit at room temperature for 2 hours or until it doubles in size.

2. Transfer the bowl of dough to the refrigerator and let it rest overnight or for 8 hours.

3. Lightly flour a work surface and, using a bench scraper or spatula, scrape the dough onto the floured surface. Sprinkle with a little more flour and fold the dough over itself a few times. Shape the dough into a ball and transfer to a piece of floured parchment paper, placing the dough seam side down. Invert the bowl you used for proofing and place it over the ball of dough, allowing the dough to rise for 1 hour or until it doubles in size.

4. Half an hour before the dough is ready, place a covered medium Dutch oven (4 to 6 quarts/3.8 to 5.7 L) inside the oven and preheat to 450°F (230°C). When the dough is ready, carefully remove the pot from the oven and, using the parchment paper, lift the ball of dough into the hot pot. Tuck the parchment paper into the pot and, using a sharp knife, cut a deep slit into the middle of the ball of dough.

5. Cover the pot and bake for 30 minutes. Remove the lid and bake for another 15 to 25 minutes or until the bread is crusty and golden brown on top. The internal temperature of the bread should be approximately 190°F (85°C). Remove the pot from the oven and let cool in the pot for at least 30 minutes before slicing the bread.

HONEY, THYME, AND CHEDDAR
SKILLET CORNBREAD

Serves 6 to 8 as a side

Hot cornbread has long been a favourite dinner accompaniment, and I often serve it with soups, stews, and chilis, as well as with grilled meats and vegetables. Whenever I wonder what I can add to a meal to bulk it up a bit, the answer is almost always cornbread. Leftovers can quickly be turned into crave-worthy croutons for salad by cubing and cooking the cornbread in the same skillet with a little butter or oil until the sides are golden and crisp. I've also gone a little crazy and made multiple batches for use in our holiday turkey stuffing.

⅓ cup (75 mL) unsalted butter

1 cup (250 mL) all-purpose flour

1 cup (250 mL) yellow cornmeal

1 tablespoon (15 mL) baking powder

1 teaspoon (5 mL) kosher salt

⅓ cup (75 mL) liquid honey

1 cup (250 mL) milk

1 large egg

1 cup (250 mL) grated aged cheddar
   (about 4 ounces/110 g)

2 sprigs thyme, leaves stripped

1. Preheat the oven to 425°F (220°C). Place the butter in a 10-inch (25 cm) cast iron skillet and slide it into the oven, letting the butter melt and begin to brown as the oven preheats.

2. In a medium bowl, combine the flour, cornmeal, baking powder, and salt; set aside.

3. In a second medium bowl, whisk together the honey, milk, and egg. When the butter has melted (watch it closely to make sure it doesn't burn), remove the skillet from the oven and stir the melted butter into the milk mixture; whisk to combine. Pour the buttermilk mixture into the dry ingredients, and add the cheddar and thyme. Mix until just combined.

4. Pour the batter into the skillet and return to the oven. Bake until the edges are browned and a skewer inserted into the centre comes out clean, 17 to 20 minutes. Remove the skillet from the oven and let cool for 10 minutes. Serve the cornbread directly from the pan.

TIP: Cornbread is best served on the day it's made, as it dries out quickly.

CHEESY GARLIC AND GREEN ONION PULL-APART BREAD

Serves 4 to 6

⅓ cup (85 mL) olive oil, plus extra for
   aluminum foil

4 small cloves garlic, grated or pressed

1 green onion, ends trimmed and
   minced

1 teaspoon (5 mL) dried dill

½ teaspoon (2 mL) dried oregano

½ teaspoon (2 mL) dried basil

½ teaspoon (2 mL) kosher salt

1 loaf round bread (about 1 pound/
   450 g)

1½ cups (375 mL) grated Oka cheese

Sometimes I like the side dish better than the main meal, and whenever this bread is on the table that's almost always the case. Cheese and bread are a winning combination, but cheese and garlic and bread is even better. I like to use a round, artisan-style loaf of bread for this recipe, as it makes an impression when you carry it to table. Rectangular loaves like ciabatta will work in a pinch, but instead of cutting the bread in a crosshatch pattern, simply make standard cuts (like slices, but not cut through to the bottom) that are about 1 inch (2.5 cm) thick.

1. Preheat the oven to 375°F (190°C). Line a rimmed sheet pan with aluminum foil and lightly brush the foil with olive oil.

2. In a small bowl, stir together the oil, garlic, green onion, dill, oregano, basil, and salt. Set aside.

3. Using a sharp bread knife, slice a 1-inch (2 cm) grid pattern into the loaf, stopping before you cut through the bottom crust of the bread. Place the bread on the prepared pan.

4. Divide the cheese evenly between the slits in the bread, and then pour the garlic oil over top, ensuring it drizzles into the crevices and soaks into the cut bread. Wrap the bread tightly in the aluminum foil and bake for 15 minutes. Remove the pan from the oven, open the foil, and return to the oven. Bake for another 10 to 15 minutes or until the cheese is melted and the bread is crispy.

5. Unwrap the bread completely and place it on a plate, platter, or cutting board to serve.

HARVEST FOCACCIA

Serves 8

Focaccia is a thick flatbread that can be eaten on its own, torn and used as a dipper, or split and stuffed to make a sandwich. I like to include pieces of focaccia in a bread basket, adding variety to the regular offerings. This recipe is the comfort food version of a basic focaccia, making it perfect for serving in the fall. Unlike most other breads, this one can be made from start to finish in just a few hours.

½ cup (125 mL) golden raisins

2 cups (500 mL) boiling water

½ teaspoon (2 mL) sugar

2¼ teaspoons (11 mL) active dry yeast

3½ cups (875 mL) all-purpose flour, plus extra for kneading

1½ teaspoons (7 mL) kosher salt, plus extra for sprinkling

1 teaspoon (5 mL) grated orange zest

2 tablespoons (30 mL) olive oil, divided

½ cup (125 mL) halved red grapes

½ cup (125 mL) crumbled goat cheese

Fresh rosemary leaves

1. In a large bowl, combine the raisins and boiling water; let soak for 15 minutes. Drain and reserve 1⅓ cups (335 mL) of the water. Return the water to the bowl and set aside the raisins. Sprinkle the sugar and yeast into the water, stir, and let stand for 5 to 10 minutes or until the mixture is foamy.

2. Add the flour, salt, orange zest, and reserved raisins to the bowl. Stir with a fork until the flour is almost completely absorbed. Using your hands, knead the dough inside the bowl until it forms a ball and is soft and sticky. Drizzle with 1 teaspoon (5 mL) oil and turn to coat, rubbing the oil over the dough. Cover the bowl with a tea towel or plastic wrap and set aside to rise in a warm spot for 1 hour or until it doubles in size.

3. Preheat the oven to 425°F (220°C). Drizzle the remaining 1 tablespoon + 2 teaspoons (25 mL) oil into a 9- × 13-inch (23 × 33 cm) enamel roasting pan. Using a bench scraper or spatula, scrape the dough into the prepared pan. Using your fingers, turn the dough over so there is oil on both sides and press it out so it fits the shape of the pan. Dimple the top of the dough, taking care not to deflate it too much. Cover and let the dough rise for another 15 minutes.

4. Press the grapes into the dough and scatter the goat cheese over top; sprinkle with rosemary and salt.

5. Bake for 20 to 25 minutes or until lightly golden on top. Cool completely or until just slightly warm. Cut into squares and serve immediately.

4 slices thick crusty bread

3 tablespoons (45 mL) olive oil, divided, plus extra for serving

Kosher salt

Freshly ground black pepper

3 cloves garlic, grated or pressed

¼ teaspoon (1 mL) crushed red pepper flakes

1 can (19 ounces/540 mL) white beans (navy or cannellini)

1 cup (250 mL) cherry tomatoes

1 tablespoon (15 mL) balsamic vinegar

Chopped fresh basil, for garnish

CHERRY TOMATO AND WHITE BEAN SKILLET BRUSCHETTA

VEGETARIAN, KID FRIENDLY, QUICK COOKING

The great artisanal toast trend of 2015 taught us that you no longer need a toaster to make fabulous toast because a cast iron skillet does an even better job of creating those coveted crispy and golden bread slices. This recipe builds on that belief and is the perfect nothing-in-the-house-to-eat weeknight dinner that doubles as a casual weekend lunch or an easy appetizer when your friends pop by for a quick visit. If you're making this bruschetta as a main dish, consider topping it with a fried egg—made in the same skillet, of course—to round out the meal.

1. Place a large cast iron, stainless steel, or non-stick skillet over medium heat. Generously brush the bread slices with 2 tablespoons (30 mL) of the oil.

2. Working in batches if necessary, cook the bread until golden brown and crisp, about 3 minutes per side. Season each side with salt and pepper. Remove from the skillet and set aside.

3. Pour the remaining 1 tablespoon (15 mL) oil into the skillet. Add the garlic and red pepper flakes and cook, stirring often, for 1 minute. Add the beans and tomatoes and cook, stirring occasionally, until slightly blistered, about 3 minutes. Add another drizzle of oil to the pan if it begins to dry out.

4. Using a fork, lightly mash some of the bean and tomato mixture. Add the balsamic vinegar, season to taste with salt and pepper, and remove the skillet from the heat.

5. Divide the tomato and bean mixture evenly over the toast and drizzle with oil. Garnish with basil and serve.

JALAPEÑO POPPER ROLLS

VEGETARIAN, MAKE AHEAD

Makes 9 large buns

I love bread and I love jalapeño poppers, and in this recipe the two marry to make the ultimate savoury bun. I like to serve these with soup in the winter, and when the weather turns warm we pack them in a picnic basket to go. My teens also like them in their school lunches in place of a regular sandwich. The method may look lengthy, but most of the work is hands-off, making this the ideal recipe for a day when you're just puttering around the house.

5 medium jalapeño peppers, halved and seeded

¾ teaspoon (4 mL) canola oil, divided

1½ cups (375 mL) warm water (110°F/45°C), divided

2¼ teaspoons (11 mL) active dry yeast

½ teaspoon (2 mL) granulated sugar

3⅓ cups (835 mL) all-purpose flour, plus extra for kneading

1 teaspoon (5 mL) kosher salt

2 tablespoons (30 mL) butter, room temperature

½ cup (125 mL) cream cheese, room temperature

2 cups (500 mL) shredded mozzarella cheese, divided

1 cup (250 mL) shredded Swiss cheese

1. Position a rack in the highest position in the oven, ideally 6 inches (15 cm) below the broiler, and cover with a piece of aluminum foil. Preheat the oven to broil.

2. Place the halved jalapeños, skin side up, directly onto the aluminum foil and broil until the skins are blistered and blackened in spots, about 10 minutes. Remove the peppers from the oven and transfer them to a bowl. Cover the bowl with a plate or plastic wrap and chill in the refrigerator for about 1 hour.

3. Meanwhile, generously grease a 10-inch (25 cm) springform pan with ½ teaspoon (2 mL) of the oil and set aside. Pour ½ cup (125 mL) of the water into a bowl (preferably that of a stand mixer) and stir in the yeast and sugar. Let sit for 5 minutes or until the mixture is foamy.

4. Add the flour, salt, butter, and remaining 1 cup (250 mL) warm water to the bowl and mix on medium speed with the dough hook (or by hand) until well combined. If the dough feels sticky, work in extra flour, 1 tablespoon (15 mL) at a time; if there are crumbs on the bottom of the bowl, add a little more water, 1 tablespoon (15 mL) at a time.

5. Continue to knead with the dough hook for another 8 minutes or until the dough is smooth and elastic. Turn the dough out onto a lightly floured work surface and knead a few times to make sure it's evenly smooth.

6. Drizzle the remaining ¼ teaspoon (1 mL) oil into the bowl. Return the dough to the bowl, and turn to coat in the oil. Cover with plastic wrap or a tea towel, and let rise in a warm place until doubled in size, about 1 hour.

Recipe continues . . .

7. Remove the peppers from the fridge and carefully peel away the skins with the edge of a knife. Discard the skins and dice the jalapeños. In a large bowl, stir together the cream cheese, 1½ cups (375 mL) of the mozzarella cheese, and ¾ cup (175 mL) of the Swiss cheese until smooth and creamy (you can do this in a stand mixer using the paddle attachment). Fold in ⅔ of the diced jalapeños, stirring until evenly mixed. Set aside.

8. Turn the risen dough out onto a lightly floured work surface and punch down to deflate. Cover the dough again and let it rest for 5 minutes. On a lightly floured work surface, roll the dough into a rectangle about 10 × 16 inches (25 × 40 cm). Spread the cream cheese and jalapeño mixture evenly over the dough to within ½ inch (1 cm) of the edges.

9. Starting with the long side closest to you, roll up the dough like a jelly roll. Cut the roll into 9 even pieces and arrange them, cut side down, in the prepared pan. Cover the pan with a tea towel and let rise until doubled in size, about 30 minutes.

10. Preheat the oven to 400°F (200°C). Uncover the rolls and sprinkle them with the remaining ½ cup (125 mL) mozzarella cheese, the remaining ¼ cup (60 mL) Swiss cheese and the reserved jalapeños. Bake for 35 minutes or until golden brown.

11. Remove the pan from the oven and let cool for 10 minutes, then carefully remove the outer ring of the springform pan and transfer the rolls to a wire rack to cool. Serve warm or at room temperature. Rolls are best consumed within 24 hours.

MINI CUBANO SANDWICHES

KID FRIENDLY, QUICK COOKING

Serves 8 to 12 as an appetizer

While I'm not sure I can claim these are authentic Cubano sand-wiches, I will assert that they are completely addictive, which is reason enough to make them. Personally, I think it's because they're simultaneously soft, crisp, sweet, and salty, not to mention impos-sibly easy to make; they really are the ideal appetizer for all your socializing needs. If you can't find deli-roasted pork, you can double up on the ham or use Genoa salami in its place. Feel free to get creative with the meat fillings, but be sure to keep the Swiss cheese, mustard, and pickles in place—they're the secret ingredients that really make these sandwiches sing.

12 soft dinner rolls
¼ cup (60 mL) yellow mustard
12 slices deli ham
12 slices deli-roasted pork
6 slices deli-style Swiss cheese
  (1 ounce/30 g each), cut in half
12 dill pickle chips
⅓ cup (85 mL) butter
1 tablespoon (15 mL) onion powder
1 tablespoon (15 mL) poppy seeds

1. Preheat the oven to 400°F (200°C). Lightly grease a 9- × 13-inch (23 × 33 cm) casserole dish with non-stick spray.

2. Without separating the rolls, cut in half horizontally and arrange the bottom half in the prepared pan. Smear 1 teaspoon (5 mL) mustard over each roll and layer with ham, pork, cheese, and pickles. Cover with the top halves of the rolls, placing them cut side down to make 1 large sandwich.

3. Melt the butter in the microwave. Stir in the onion powder and poppy seeds. Brush the butter mixture evenly over the rolls.

4. Cover the dish with foil and bake for 10 minutes. Uncover and bake for another 5 to 10 minutes or until the cheese melts and the buns are golden brown. Remove the dish from the oven and let cool for 5 minutes. Cut into 12 mini sandwiches and serve immediately.

EASY GRILLED CHEESE FOR A CROWD

VEGETARIAN, KID FRIENDLY, QUICK COOKING

Makes 8 sandwiches

This is the only recipe in the book that calls for two cooking vessels, but I don't really feel like I'm cheating because it's just two of the same pan. Sheet pans are so incredibly versatile, and here they work together as a panini press of sorts to cook several grilled sandwiches at once. Once you try this method, you'll be hard pressed to stand by the stove flipping sandwiches for a crowd again. Feel free to get creative with other fillings, such as cooked bacon, caramelized onions, or fresh tender greens. Just know that you'll need more than two sheet pans to create your sandwiches if you venture in that direction.

8 tablespoons (120 mL) mayonnaise

16 slices white or whole wheat
    sandwich bread

4 cups (1 L) coarsely grated cheese
    (I like a mix of Monterey Jack, cheddar,
    mozzarella, and Swiss)

Kosher salt

Freshly ground black pepper

1. Place 2 rimmed sheet pans, one on top of the other, in the oven and preheat to 450°F (230°C).
2. Spread 1½ teaspoons (7 mL) of mayonnaise over one side of each slice of bread. Using oven mitts, carefully remove the pre-heated sheet pans from the oven. Working quickly, place 8 slices of bread, mayonnaise side down, on one of the sheet pans. Top each slice with ½ cup (125 mL) cheese, season with salt and pepper, and cover with a piece of bread, mayonnaise side up.
3. Slide the sheet pan into the oven and place the second sheet pan on top of it, rimmed side up. Bake until the bread is golden brown and the cheese is melted, about 15 minutes.
4. Carefully remove the sheet pans from the oven. Set aside the top sheet pan and transfer the sandwiches to a cutting board. Cut the sandwiches in half and serve hot.

Serves 6

CRISPY CHICKEN SANDWICHES

For the sandwiches

¾ cup (175 mL) panko bread crumbs

1½ tablespoons (22 mL) olive oil

1 teaspoon (5 mL) kosher salt

½ teaspoon (2 mL) freshly ground
    black pepper

½ teaspoon (2 mL) smoked or sweet
    paprika

½ teaspoon (2 mL) celery seed

¼ teaspoon (1 mL) dried oregano

¼ teaspoon (1 mL) garlic powder

¼ teaspoon (1 mL) onion powder

¼ teaspoon (1 mL) dried basil

Pinch of cayenne pepper

6 boneless, skinless chicken thighs
    (about 1½ pounds/675 g)

6 English muffins, split and toasted

Thinly sliced iceberg lettuce, for
    garnish

For the sauce

¾ cup (175 mL) mayonnaise

2 tablespoons (30 mL) ketchup

1 tablespoon (15 mL) Dijon mustard

2 tablespoons (30 mL) sweet pickle
    relish

½ teaspoon (2 mL) Sriracha hot sauce

These sandwiches are so good that once you try them you'll never want to sit in a drive-thru line again. I've skipped the usual steps of dredging the chicken in flour, then egg, then bread crumbs, and instead made a flavoured bread crumb topping not unlike a popular boxed brand you may have grown up with. I use English muffins in my recipe because I like the way the craters catch the sauce, but any variety of toasted bun will work in a pinch.

1. Preheat the oven to 400°F (200°C). Line a large rimmed sheet pan with aluminum foil or parchment paper and top with a wire rack. Lightly mist the rack with non-stick spray; set aside.

2. In a large resealable plastic bag, add the panko, oil, salt, pepper, paprika, celery seed, oregano, garlic powder, onion powder, basil, and cayenne. Seal the bag and shake until well combined and the crumbs look like wet sand.

3. Using tongs, drop 2 pieces of chicken into the bag. Seal and shake until chicken is evenly covered in the crumb mixture. Remove, shake off the excess crumbs, and arrange on the prepared rack. Repeat with the remaining chicken thighs. Bake until golden brown, crispy, and cooked through, about 25 minutes.

4. Meanwhile, to make the sauce, add the mayonnaise, ketchup, mustard, relish, and Sriracha to a bowl and whisk to combine. Chill until ready to serve.

5. To make the sandwiches, spread both sides of each English muffin with the sauce. Place a piece of chicken on the bottom bun, top with heaps of lettuce, and cover with the top bun. Serve immediately.

GRILLED APPLE AND BRIE SANDWICHES

VEGETARIAN, KID FRIENDLY, QUICK COOKING

Makes 4 sandwiches

I could eat this sandwich every day, but sadly my waistline—not to mention my heart—doesn't quite agree. Instead, we save them for Saturday lunches in the fall, serving them alongside a bowl of seasonal soup. I dare say this might be one of the most delicious rituals you'll find in this book.

1. In a small bowl, combine the butter and thyme and mix well; set aside.
2. Heat a medium or large cast iron, stainless steel, or non-stick skillet over medium-low heat. Depending on the size of the pan, you may have to cook the sandwiches in batches.
3. To assemble the sandwiches, lay 8 slices of bread out on a counter or large cutting board and divide the mayonnaise evenly over one side of each slice. Set 4 slices of bread mayonnaise side up, and top each with 2 slices of brie, 3 to 4 apple slices, ¼ cup (60 mL) arugula, and ¼ cup (60 mL) cheddar. Then cover each with a slice of bread, mayonnaise side down.
4. Smear the thyme-infused butter over the outsides of the sandwiches (both sides) and transfer to the hot skillet. Cook each sandwich for 2 to 3 minutes per side or until the cheese is melted and the bread is golden brown. Allow to cool for 1 minute before slicing sandwiches in half.

4 tablespoons (60 mL) butter, room temperature
1 teaspoon (5 mL) fresh thyme leaves
¼ cup (60 mL) mayonnaise
8 slices thick-cut sourdough bread (or any crusty bread)
8 slices thick-cut brie cheese
1 large apple (Honeycrisp or Granny Smith), cored and thinly sliced
1 cup (250 mL) arugula leaves
1 cup (250 mL) grated aged cheddar cheese

PERSONAL PAN-FRIED PIZZA, TWO WAYS

Each pizza serves 1

For the spinach and egg pizza

½ teaspoon (2 mL) olive oil

1 large (10 inches/25 cm) tortilla

¼ cup (60 mL) basil pesto

8 thin slices fresh mozzarella

1 cup (250 mL) baby spinach leaves

2 tablespoons (30 mL) crumbled feta cheese

Pinch of crushed red pepper flakes

1 large egg (optional)

Kosher salt

Freshly ground black pepper

Chopped fresh chives, for garnish

For the pizza margherita

½ teaspoon (2 mL) olive oil

1 large (10 inches/25 cm) tortilla

¼ cup (60 mL) Pantry Pizza Sauce (page 247) or store-bought marinara sauce

8 thin slices fresh mozzarella

Fresh basil leaves, for garnish

Easier than takeout, these personal pan pizzas are a cheater's version for people who love thin crusts. The cast iron skillet is essential here, as it aids in crisping the bottom of the tortilla. Choose a pan that's close in diameter to your tortilla, so it fits snugly in the bottom. The sides of the skillet will help to hold the toppings in place since tortillas don't have a puffy crust to prevent the cheese and toppings from sliding off.

SPINACH AND EGG PIZZA

1. Position a rack in the highest position in the oven, ideally 6 inches (15 cm) below the broiler, and preheat the oven to broil.

2. In a cast iron skillet, heat the oil over medium heat until it shimmers, and then brush it evenly over the bottom and sides of the skillet. Add the tortilla and cover it with the pesto, spreading it all the way to the edges. Top with the mozzarella, spinach, and feta. Sprinkle with the red pepper flakes. Crack the egg over top, if using, taking care not to break the yolk. Season with salt and pepper to taste.

3. Transfer the skillet to the oven and broil until the cheese is melted and beginning to brown and the egg is cooked but still a little runny, about 2 to 3 minutes.

4. Using a metal spatula, gently pry the pizza from the edges of the skillet. If the bottom of the tortilla isn't crisp enough, return the skillet to the stovetop and cook over medium-high heat until the desired crispness is achieved. Slide the pizza onto a cutting board, garnish with the chives, cut, and serve immediately.

PIZZA MARGHERITA

1. Position a rack in the highest position in the oven, ideally 6 inches (15 cm) below the broiler, and preheat the oven to broil.

2. In a cast iron skillet, heat the oil over medium heat until it shimmers, and then brush it evenly over the bottom and sides of the skillet. Add the tortilla and cover it with the sauce, spreading it all the way to the edges. Top with the mozzarella, spacing the slices evenly over the surface of the tortilla. Transfer the skillet to the oven and broil until the cheese is melted, about 1 to 2 minutes.

3. Using a metal spatula, gently pry the pizza from the edges of the skillet. If the bottom of the tortilla isn't crisp enough, return the skillet to the stovetop and cook over medium-high heat until the desired crispness is achieved. Slide the pizza onto a cutting board, garnish with the basil, cut, and serve immediately.

PEACH, PROSCIUTTO, AND BRIE FLATBREAD

Serves 4

I've long wondered if there really is a difference between flatbread and pizza, and here's my conclusion: kind of, but not really. Pizzas typically follow the formula of crust, sauce, cheese, and toppings, but flatbreads tend to be a little more experimental. Both can be made from rolled and stretched dough, but I've taken a shortcut here and used store-bought naan for my base. Usually located in the bakery or deli section of a grocery store, naan is a leavened, oven-baked flatbread that often can be purchased in packages of two or four.

1. Preheat the oven to 400°F (200°C) and line a rimmed sheet pan with parchment paper.
2. Spread the preserves onto the naan, dividing it evenly between the pieces of bread. Layer each flatbread with prosciutto, brie, peach, and red onion, dividing the ingredients evenly between the pieces of naan. Season with pepper.
3. Bake for 10 to 13 minutes or until the edges of the naan are golden and the cheese is melted. Sprinkle with fresh basil, cut into pieces if desired, and serve.

VARIATION: If peaches are not in season, you can replace them with sliced apples.

½ cup (125 mL) peach or apricot preserves

4 pieces (each 7 inches/18 cm wide) naan bread

8 thin slices prosciutto, torn into pieces

4 ounces (110 g) brie cheese, thinly sliced

2 small ripe peaches, pitted and thinly sliced

¼ small red onion, thinly sliced

Freshly ground black pepper

Fresh basil, for garnish

TIP: You can also use mini naan for this recipe. They are typically 3 inches (8 cm) wide, so you'll be able to make 8 flatbreads with the ingredients in the recipe. Large pieces of naan make this a complete meal, while smaller pieces are better as an appetizer.

BARBECUE CHICKPEA PIZZA

VEGETARIAN, MAKE AHEAD, KID FRIENDLY

For the pizza dough

1½ cups (375 mL) warm water
  (110°F/45°C)

2¼ teaspoons (11 mL) active dry yeast

¾ teaspoon (4 mL) sugar

3 tablespoons + 1 teaspoon (50 mL)
  olive oil, divided

1 teaspoon (5 mL) salt

3¾ to 4 cups (925 mL to 1 L) all-purpose
  flour, divided

For the topping

½ cup + 2 tablespoons (155 mL)
  barbecue sauce, divided

1 can (19 ounces/540 mL) chickpeas,
  drained and rinsed

1½ cups (375 mL) shredded mozzarella
  cheese

1½ cups (375 mL) shredded aged
  cheddar cheese

½ small red onion, thinly sliced

Fresh cilantro, for garnish

My family loves barbecue chicken pizza, but I'm always looking for ways to make more of our meals meatless, which is how this chickpea pizza came to be. It might seem unusual to use legumes on a pizza, but I promise it works. My kids are huge fans, as is everyone else who's tasted it, and because the dough needs to be made the night before, preparing the actual pizza can be done in fifteen minutes flat if you're using canned chickpeas.

1. To make the pizza dough, in a large bowl, stir together the water, yeast, and sugar. Set aside for 5 minutes or until the mixture is foamy. (If the yeast doesn't bubble, toss it out, purchase new yeast, and start over.)

2. Using a wooden spoon, stir in 2 tablespoons (30 mL) oil, salt, and 3½ cups (875 mL) flour. Mix until the dough comes together and is shaggy. Sprinkle the counter with more flour, tip the dough onto the work surface, and knead for 5 to 10 minutes, using as much of the remaining flour as needed to create a dough that's soft and springy. Lightly oil a clean bowl (or wash the bowl you used to mix the dough) with 1 teaspoon (5 mL) oil. Place the pizza dough in the bowl and cover the bowl with plastic wrap. Store in the refrigerator for 12 to 18 hours.

3. When you are ready to make the pizza, preheat the oven to 500°F (260°C). Brush the remaining 1 tablespoon (15 mL) oil over a 13- × 18-inch (33 × 45 cm) sheet pan. Using your hands, stretch the pizza dough over the pan, pressing it into the corners and up the sides.

4. In a medium bowl, toss 2 tablespoons (30 mL) barbecue sauce with the chickpeas to coat; set aside. Spread the remaining ½ cup (125 mL) barbecue sauce over the pizza dough. Layer on the mozzarella cheese, chickpeas, cheddar cheese, and red onion, covering the pizza evenly.

5. Carefully slide the sheet pan into the oven. Bake for 14 to 16 minutes or until the pizza crust is golden brown along the edges and the cheeses are melted. Remove the sheet pan from the oven and let cool for 5 minutes. Sprinkle with fresh cilantro, cut into squares, and serve.

MUFFIN PAN
TUNA MELTS

I'm not a fan of warm tuna sandwiches, but the same cannot be said for my kids, who love tuna melts for lunch. I try to understand their affection because what's not to love about oozy, melted cheese and crisp, golden toast and tuna dolled up with mustard, mayonnaise, and lemon juice? Making these in a muffin tin is a fun twist on an otherwise classic creation; if you have little ones, they will have fun measuring and mixing the ingredients to make these sandwiches with you.

1. Preheat the oven to 375°F (190°C). Lightly butter a standard 12-cup muffin tin with 3 tablespoons (45 mL) of the melted butter. Brush the remaining 3 tablespoons (45 mL) butter over one side of the bread slices and press the bread into the prepared muffin cups, buttered sides up.
2. In a medium bowl, break up the tuna with a fork. Stir in the celery, onion, mayonnaise, mustard, pepper, lemon zest, and lemon juice. Season with salt to taste.
3. Spoon 2 to 3 tablespoons (30 to 45 mL) of the tuna mixture into each bread-lined muffin cup. Top with the Monterey Jack, dividing the cheese evenly between the 12 cups.
4. Bake for 10 to 13 minutes or until the filling is hot and the cheese is bubbling. Remove the muffin tin from the oven and let cool for 5 minutes. Garnish the melts with dill sprigs and serve immediately.

Makes 12 melts; serves 4 to 6 adults
or 6 to 12 children

6 tablespoons (90 mL) unsalted butter, melted, divided

12 slices whole wheat bread, crusts removed

2 cans (6 ounces/170 g each) chunk white tuna packed in water, drained

2 tablespoons (30 mL) minced celery

2 tablespoons (30 mL) minced red onion

⅓ cup (85 mL) mayonnaise

1 tablespoon (15 mL) whole grain mustard

½ teaspoon (2 mL) freshly ground black pepper

Zest and juice of ½ lemon

Kosher salt

¾ cup (175 mL) grated Monterey Jack cheese

Fresh dill sprigs, for garnish

MEDITERRANEAN SOCCA PIZZA

MAKE AHEAD, KID FRIENDLY, QUICK COOKING, GLUTEN-FREE, VEGETARIAN

Serves 2 to 4

1 cup (250 mL) chickpea flour

1 cup (250 mL) water

4 tablespoons (60 mL) olive oil, divided

1 teaspoon (5 mL) kosher salt

1 teaspoon (5 mL) freshly ground black pepper

½ cup (125 mL) grated mozzarella cheese

1 small zucchini, thinly sliced or peeled into ribbons

6 pitted kalamata or green olives, halved

¼ cup (60 mL) crumbled feta cheese

½ teaspoon (2 mL) dried oregano

Just when I thought I knew about all the pizza variations, I stumbled upon socca, a pizza-like pancake made from chickpea flour and water. A popular European street food, it's often served unadorned with nothing more than a sprinkling of salt and pepper and maybe a few fresh herbs. This version turns it into more of a Mediterranean pizza topped with soft zucchini ribbons, salty olives, and crumbled feta. A few years ago you may have had to traipse to a specialty food store to find the gluten-free chickpea flour, but today it's available in many larger grocery stores and almost all bulk food stores.

1. Position a rack in the top third of the oven and preheat to broil.
2. In a medium bowl, whisk together the flour, water, 3 tablespoons (45 mL) oil, salt, and pepper. Set aside for 30 minutes.
3. In a 10-inch (25 cm) skillet, heat the remaining 1 tablespoon (15 mL) oil over medium-high heat, and then swirl it around the skillet. Add the batter and cook for 5 to 7 minutes or until the top is almost set and the edges are beginning to pull away from the sides of the skillet. Flip the socca and cook for 1 minute more.
4. Sprinkle the mozzarella over the socca. Top with the zucchini, olives, and feta. Sprinkle with the oregano.
5. Place the skillet in the oven and cook for 1 to 2 minutes or until the cheese is melted and browned in spots and the sooca is crisp. Remove the skillet from the oven and let cool for 2 to 3 minutes before slicing. Serve immediately or at room temperature.

SIMPLE MEAT-LOVER'S DEEP-DISH PIZZA

Serves 4

I like the idea of designating certain nights of the week to eating specific foods. We often go meatless on Mondays and tuck into tacos on Tuesdays. I appreciate that this way of eating almost allows me to be lazy in my meal planning. It takes the guesswork out of what to make for dinner on certain days and makes grocery shopping easier because I keep certain pantry and fridge basics on hand all the time. Friday is definitely pizza night in our house, and we try to keep it interesting by switching up the type of pizza we cook. Sometimes it's a regular sheet pan variety, and other times we make Salami Stromboli (page 110), but the one we love the most is this deep-dish style. The billowy crust is ideal for holding whatever toppings you choose, and while you can really use a mix of both proteins and vegetables, I ultimately recommend using whatever leftovers you have kicking around in the fridge for the filling. By using pre-cooked ingredients, this is a true one-pan meal.

1. To make the pizza dough, combine the yeast, sugar, and water in the bowl of a stand mixer and let rest for 5 minutes or until the mixture is foamy.
2. Add the oil, 2 cups (500 mL) flour, and salt to the bowl. Mix with the dough hook at medium-low speed until smooth. Turn the dough out onto a lightly floured surface and knead until smooth and elastic, gradually adding in as much of the remaining flour as needed.
3. Place the dough in a large, lightly oiled bowl and cover. Allow the dough to rise in a warm place for 1½ hours or until doubled in size.
4. Preheat the oven to 425°F (220°C). Coat the bottom and sides of a 10-inch (25 cm) springform pan with oil. Punch the dough down and turn it out onto a lightly floured surface. Using your fingers, press the dough into a 13-inch (33 cm) circle. Carefully lift the dough into the prepared pan, pressing it into the bottom and halfway up the sides.
5. Spread the sauce or pesto over the dough and top with your chosen meat and veggies. Sprinkle the mozzarella and Parmesan cheeses over top. Scatter the oregano over the entire pizza. Bake for 25 to 28 minutes or until the crust and cheese are golden brown. Remove the pan from the oven and let cool for 5 minutes, then release the pizza from the pan by removing the outer ring. Garnish the pizza with basil, if using, cut into 6 wedges, and serve.

For the pizza dough

1¼ teaspoon (6 mL) yeast

½ teaspoon (2 mL) sugar

¾ cup (175 mL) warm water

3 tablespoons (45 mL) olive oil, plus extra for the pan

2 to 2¼ cups (500 to 560 mL) all-purpose flour, divided

½ teaspoon (2 mL) kosher salt

For the filling

¾ cup (175 mL) marinara sauce, pizza sauce, or pesto

1½ cups (375 mL) cooked meat (like crumbled bacon, shredded rotisserie chicken, salami, pepperoni, etc.)

1½ cups (375 mL) grated mozzarella cheese

¼ cup (60 mL) grated Parmesan cheese

1 teaspoon (5 mL) dried oregano

Fresh basil, for garnish (optional)

VARIATION: To make this pizza vegetarian, feel free to replace equal quantities of meat with any leftover cooked vegetables you have in the refrigerator.

Serves 4

3 teaspoons (15 mL) olive oil, divided

½ batch Pizza Dough (page 104) or
    1 ball store-bought pizza dough

½ cup (125 mL) Pantry Pizza Sauce
    (page 247), Roasted Tomato Sauce
    (page 244), or store-bought tomato
    sauce, plus extra for dipping

1 teaspoon (5 mL) dried oregano, plus
    extra for garnish

¼ to ½ teaspoon (1 to 2 mL) crushed
    red pepper flakes

2 cups (500 mL) grated mozzarella
    cheese

9 slices salami

12 to 16 slices pepperoni

½ cup (125 mL) grated Parmesan
    cheese

Sea salt, for garnish

SALAMI STROMBOLI

MAKE AHEAD, KID FRIENDLY

Stromboli is made by rolling up pizza dough with toppings into a cylinder before baking it. The result is a crispy turnover stuffed with meat, cheese, and tomato sauce—and it's utterly delicious. Once cut into pieces, stromboli can be eaten like pizza or served on a platter like a sandwich. My middle son's birthday is at the end of January, and it's not uncommon for us to serve steaming pots of soup alongside wedges of stromboli with Roasted Tomato Sauce (page 244) for dipping. It's a crowd-pleasing dinner the entire extended family loves. If using the Barbecue Chickpea Pizza dough recipe on page 104, be sure to make it the night before. Otherwise, feel free to use a ball of pizza dough purchased from your favourite grocery store or bakery.

1. Position a rack in the top third of the oven and preheat to 350°F (180°C). Brush 2 teaspoons (10 mL) oil over a rimmed sheet pan and, using your hands, stretch the pizza dough over the pan, pressing it as far into the corners as possible.

2. Spread pizza sauce over the dough, leaving a 2-inch (5 cm) border around the edges. Sprinkle with the oregano and red pepper flakes. Top with the mozzarella, salami, pepperoni, and Parmesan.

3. Very carefully, so as not to tear the dough, roll up the pizza dough like a jelly roll, starting with one long side. Brush the entire rolled stromboli with the remaining 1 teaspoon (5 mL) oil and sprinkle with a pinch each of oregano and sea salt. Cut slits in the top of the dough for venting, and bake for 45 to 60 minutes or until golden brown.

4. Remove the sheet pan from the oven and let cool for 5 minutes, then cut into 1½-inch (4 cm) thick pieces. Serve with extra pizza sauce for dipping.

VARIATION: To make a vegetarian stromboli, omit the salami and pepperoni and substitute with half of a sliced medium red onion and 1 package (10 ounces/280 g) frozen chopped spinach or kale (thawed and squeezed, with no visible liquid remaining).

TURKEY LENTIL SLOPPY JOES WITH QUICK CABBAGE SLAW

Serves 8

My brother-in-law owns a restaurant called Sloppy Joes, but unfortunately this recipe isn't the one he serves from his commercial kitchen. He keeps that one, plus at least thirty others, stored in a top secret vault (his brain!) despite our best efforts to get him to share just a few. Although this version isn't being served to the general public, I think my take on this popular sandwich is worthy of sharing. Lightened up with a mix of ground turkey and fibrous lentils, you can easily double or triple this recipe for a party. The slaw adds some crunch to this dish. Its simplicity lends itself well to customization, so feel free to play around with vegetables if you like, maybe adding some grated apple or green cabbage to the mix.

1. In a large cast iron, stainless steel, or non-stick skillet, heat the oil over medium heat. Add the onions, season with a generous pinch of salt and sauté until soft and translucent, about 3 to 5 minutes. Add the garlic and cook for 1 minute more. Crumble the ground turkey into the skillet and stir to combine, cooking until browned. Add the lentils, chili powder, oregano, cumin, pepper, and tomato paste and stir, cooking for another 1 to 2 minutes to infuse the turkey and lentils with the spices.

2. Stir in the crushed tomatoes, brown sugar, mustard, Worcestershire, and hot sauce. Reduce the heat to medium-low and simmer, partially covered, for 20 minutes. Check seasonings and add more salt if needed.

3. While the meat mixture is cooking, make the slaw. Place the cabbage in a medium bowl and, using a vegetable peeler, shave the carrot into ribbons. Add carrot and green onions to the bowl and toss with your hands to combine.

4. In a small bowl, whisk together the mayonnaise, lime juice, honey, and celery seed. Pour over the cabbage and toss to combine. Finish with a generous pinch of salt.

5. Spoon the Sloppy Joes onto the toasted rolls. Top with the slaw and serve at once.

For the Sloppy Joes

2 tablespoons (30 mL) olive oil

1 small onion, finely chopped (about ½ cup/125 mL)

Kosher salt

2 cloves garlic, grated or pressed

1 pound (450 g) ground turkey

2 cups (500 mL) cooked green or brown lentils (or one 19-ounce/ 540 mL can, rinsed and drained)

3 tablespoons (45 mL) chili powder

1 teaspoon (5 mL) dried oregano

1 teaspoon (5 mL) ground cumin

½ teaspoon (2 mL) freshly ground black pepper

2 tablespoons (30 mL) tomato paste

1 can (28 ounces/796 mL) crushed tomatoes

3 tablespoons (45 mL) brown sugar

1 tablespoon (15 mL) prepared yellow mustard

1 teaspoon (5 mL) Worcestershire sauce

1 teaspoon (5 mL) hot sauce

For the slaw

4 cups (1 L) chopped red cabbage (about 1 small cabbage)

1 large carrot, peeled

3 green onions, ends trimmed and thinly sliced

½ cup (125 mL) mayonnaise

¼ cup (60 mL) fresh lime juice

2 teaspoons (10 mL) liquid honey

1 teaspoon (5 mL) celery seed

Kosher salt

For serving

8 whole wheat dinner rolls or hamburger buns (split in half and toasted)

SKILLET 101: THE KIND OF
HEAVY METAL EVERYONE ENJOYS

A well-equipped kitchen probably has several types of skillets, such as non-stick, cast iron, enamel-coated, and stainless steel. Stainless steel skillets heat relatively evenly and are considered an "everyday" pan for jobs like cooking stir-fries and simmering sauces. Cast iron pans, on the other hand, take longer to reach the desired level of heat but hold it better than the stainless steel kind and can achieve that coveted golden brown crust on a piece of meat like steak. Although these pans can be used interchangeably, I more often cook with my cast iron skillets than my stainless steel ones. I'm not partial to non-stick skillets, and rarely use mine, but I have included them in the recipes because I know how popular they are. I also believe that they are an excellent starter pan for kids learning to cook at home.

WHAT TO LOOK FOR

Available in a variety of sizes, each skillet has its merits and every cook has a preference, but you'll want to look for some universal features when purchasing one of these pans for your kitchen. Heavy-bottomed, long-handled, oven-safe skillets are essential for making dishes like Spicy Corn and Bacon Frittata (page 21), where you start out on the stovetop and finish in the oven. Cast iron pans are excellent for baking desserts (Salted Chocolate Tahini Skillet Blondies on page 210) and breads (Honey, Thyme, and Cheddar Skillet Cornbread on page 83), as the hot bottom and high sides of a well-seasoned pan create the crispy golden crust we often look for in a baked good. Other dishes, like Skillet Gnocchi with Bacon and Peas (page 156), require a quick blast under the broiler, so you want to make sure you use a pan than can safely handle the high heat.

CAST IRON SKILLETS: Sturdier than a regular skillet, the secret to making a cast iron skillet work for you is to use it as often as possible. The more it is used, the better its seasoning will be, which results in creating a non-stick finish of sorts on the bottom of the pan. Naturally, this translates to better and easier cooking. 10- and 12-inch (20 to 25 cm) skillets are ideal for most recipes, so if you're purchasing one for the first time, I'd recommend this size. If you have a large family, or cook for big groups, you may want to invest in a 14-inch (35 cm) skillet. Generally speaking, cast iron skillets are relatively inexpensive and can be purchased for less than $40. If you plan on baking a lot of desserts in these skillets—and I encourage you to do so—you may want to invest in two: one for savoury recipes and the other for sweet creations. Cast iron is designed to hold on to the "seasoning" and I feel confident you don't want your skillet desserts to taste like the steak you seared.

STAINLESS STEEL SKILLETS: The nice thing about stainless steel is that it doesn't dent, chip, rust, or scratch easily. It also doesn't react with acidic foods (like cast iron) and is generally very easy to clean. Popular pans in this category can cost upwards of $150. If you aren't quite ready to invest more than a hundred dollars in a stainless steel skillet, rest assured there are some dependable budget picks available for around $50. While it may be tempting to make your skillet purchase online, I suggest visiting a kitchen store so you can get a feel for handle comfort—all pans are not created equally.

NON-STICK SKILLETS: The market for non-stick skillets is crowded and full of options. Made with a classic coating like Teflon or more modern, eco-friendly alternatives like ceramic and porcelain, finding a pan you like shouldn't be too difficult.

Whichever type of skillet you choose, know that slope-sided pans make it easy to move food around in the skillet, preventing anything from getting stuck in the corners. They also encourage evaporation and browning, while straight-sided pans trap moisture and are best for slower cooking, such as braising.

CARING FOR AND CLEANING SKILLETS

CAST IRON SKILLETS: This type of skillet requires seasoning before use. Nowadays, most pans come preseasoned, but if yours didn't—or you need to re-season it—the process is simple. Drizzle ½ teaspoon (2 mL) or so of vegetable or flax oil (don't use olive oil) into the pan and wipe it around with a paper towel. Bake the skillet in the oven at 400°F (200°C) for 30 minutes. Remove the skillet from the oven, let cool, and repeat the process three or four times. That's honestly all it takes! Clean your pans well after each use. It's always best to use the least aggressive option available when caring for your cast iron skillet. This means that if you can wipe it clean with a piece of paper towel, do so. If you need to use some water and a gentle brush to remove caked-on food, that also works well. For a more abrasive cleaning, drizzle some olive oil into the pan and add a handful of kosher salt. Scrub the salt and oil into the pan with a wad of paper towel. The salt will collect the dirt and the pan will get clean. Discard the salt and wipe the pan clean. Despite conventional wisdom, you *can* clean these pans with mild dish soap and warm water. What you can't do is let them soak in a sink full of soapy water. So, wipe or wash the pan clean, thoroughly dry it with a tea towel or paper towel, and season it again with a little oil. You don't need to bake it in the oven; just set the pan on a burner, rub a little oil into the skillet, and continue heating the pan until it smokes. Then wipe it once more, let cool, and put it away. Enamel-coated cast iron pans need a little less attention, and although they are dishwasher safe, it's best to wash them by hand with warm soapy water and a nylon scrub brush.

STAINLESS STEEL SKILLETS: Less fussy than cast iron skillets, these really need nothing more than a solid soak in warm soapy water to remove caked-on food. Use non-abrasive cleaners and sponges to avoid damaging the surface of the pan. To remove burnt-on food, cover the bottom of the pan with baking soda, then cover with water. Bring to a boil, scraping the debris from the pan with a wooden spoon, then wash the pan as you normally would. This will remove the burnt-on food and the "rainbow" look spotted on some stainless steel. Thoroughly dry stainless steel cookware to avoid water spots; if they appear, lightly wet the area of the pan and gently scrub with a sponge sprinkled with baking soda. As always, consult the manufacturer's instructions for more information.

NON-STICK SKILLETS: These skillets should be handwashed in warm, soapy water, as high heat and harsh detergents can ruin their non-stick coatings. This type of cookware is prone to pitting and peeling after frequent use, which means that it's time for the skillet to be discarded.

HOW TO STORE

I store my washed and thoroughly dried cast iron and stainless steel skillets nestled inside of each other. Non-stick skillets can also be stored this way, but should have a piece of paper towel between them to protect their coating. If you have the room, it's ideal to hang them from a pot rack or on a wall.

TOP TIPS FOR USE

- Always preheat a skillet before adding food to it, and if using, heat the oil before adding other ingredients. Make sure the skillet has reached at least medium heat before adding ingredients to the pan, otherwise your food (specifically meat) will stick to the pan, leading to uneven cooking.

- Do not rush the heating process. Because both cast iron and stainless steel skillets hold their heat well, they're at risk of overheating and should be warmed slowly to avoid burning food.

- Don't overcrowd the skillet or the food will be more likely to steam rather than brown; cook in batches if necessary.

- Cook food in a single layer and leave some space between the items to allow liquid to evaporate.
- Meat and vegetables should be cut into similar-size pieces for even cooking.
- The easiest way to tell if your skillet is hot enough is to use a good old-fashioned water test: flick some water on the pan; if it just sits there, the pan's not hot enough yet. If it sizzles and evaporates within a couple of seconds, the pan should be good to go. If it combines into a ball and skates around the pan, the pan's too hot, so bring down the temperature before you add the oil. Another way to tell if your skillet is too hot is to look at the oil. It should be shimmering, not smoking.

MAIN MEALS

SIMPLE ENOUGH FOR everyday dinner, but special enough for guests, main meals made in one pot are not to be underestimated. They deliver big flavour, desired textures, and far less cleanup than ordinary dinners. They meet the needs of the modern, busy cook who craves healthy, mindful meals but all too often sacrifices such things because of a demanding calendar or schedule. You can create comfort in the form of a homemade meal by using a variety of cooking vessels and simple cooking techniques. These dinners—such as Baked Risotto with Chicken, Leeks, and Lemon (page 120), Crispy Black Bean Tacos (page 152), and One-Pot Baked Beefaroni (page 142)—are the satisfying solution a home cook needs to make effortless, tasty meals a reality.

BAKED RISOTTO WITH CHICKEN, LEEKS, AND LEMON

MAKE AHEAD, KID FRIENDLY, GLUTEN-FREE

Serves 4 to 6

8 bone-in, skin-on chicken thighs (excess skin and fat removed), at room temperature

Kosher salt

Freshly ground black pepper

1 teaspoon (5 mL) olive oil

2 leeks (about 1 inch/2 cm in diameter each), root ends and dark green tops removed, sliced in half lengthwise and then cut crosswise in ½-inch (1 cm) thick pieces (about 2 cups/ 500 mL)

1 cup (250 mL) arborio rice

¼ cup (60 mL) dry white wine

1 small lemon, scrubbed and thinly sliced

2 cups (500 mL) Whole Chicken Broth (page 48) or low-sodium store-bought chicken broth

For serving (optional)

Freshly grated Parmesan cheese

Finely chopped fresh chives

Oh, I love this dish. It's perfect to serve at the beginning of spring, when the weather still has you craving comfort food, but the thought of finding another root vegetable on your dinner plate leaves you feeling glum. The leeks and lemon lighten this dish, and if you want to infuse more spring flavours, you can add 1 to 2 cups (250 to 500 mL) of peas to the rice before baking it. Make sure you use a broth whose taste you enjoy. If I don't have homemade broth on hand, I'm partial to using a broth paste like the Better Than Bouillon brand.

1. Preheat the oven to 400°F (200°C).
2. Pat the chicken thighs dry with a paper towel and season generously with salt and pepper. In a 12-inch (30 cm) oven-safe cast iron, stainless steel, or non-stick skillet, heat the oil over medium-high heat. Add the chicken, skin side down, cooking until the skin is golden and crisp, about 8 minutes. (Be patient here, as you won't be able to flip the chicken without resistance until the skin is sufficiently browned.) Flip the chicken pieces and brown the second side, cooking for another 2 minutes. Transfer the chicken to a plate and set aside.
3. Add the leeks and rice to the skillet, season to taste with salt and pepper, and stir. Add the wine and stir again, scraping up the browned bits from the bottom of the skillet and cooking until the rice has absorbed most of the liquid.
4. Return the chicken, skin side up, and any accumulated juices to the skillet. Tuck the lemon slices around the chicken. Pour the broth over top. The rice should be covered and most of the chicken should be submerged, with the exception of the skin.
5. Transfer the skillet to the oven and bake until the rice is tender and creamy and the chicken is cooked through, 35 to 40 minutes. Remove the skillet from the oven and let stand for 5 minutes. Sprinkle with the Parmesan cheese and chives, if using, and serve directly from the skillet.

TIP: To clean the leeks, place the sliced leeks in a bowl of cold water and use your fingers to agitate the slices, releasing any dirt that's clinging to them. Using a slotted spoon or sieve, move the leeks to a colander to drain.

FLAT ROASTED CHICKEN WITH FARRO

MAKE AHEAD, KID FRIENDLY, WHOLE GRAIN

Serves 4 to 6

When choosing which roasted chicken dish to include in this book, I knew I had to go with one that delivered an entire dinner to the table. I love the pairing of roasted chicken with whole grains, so I homed in on that and came up with this Italian-inspired feast. Don't skimp on the red wine vinegar at the end; I'm convinced it's what makes this whole meal sing.

1 medium onion, finely chopped

2 small carrots, finely diced

2 celery stalks, finely diced

3 cloves garlic, grated or pressed

½ cup (125 mL) finely chopped tomatoes

2 sprigs thyme, leaves stripped, divided

1½ cups (375 mL) farro, well rinsed and drained

Kosher salt

Freshly ground black pepper

3 cups (750 mL) Whole Chicken Broth (page 48) or low-sodium store-bought chicken broth

1 tablespoon (30 mL) tomato paste

1 whole chicken (3 to 4 pounds/1.4 to 1.8 kg)

2 tablespoons (30 mL) butter, divided

½ teaspoon (2 mL) dried oregano

¼ teaspoon (1 mL) crushed red pepper flakes

2 bay leaves

2 teaspoons (10 mL) red wine vinegar

1. Preheat the oven to 400°F (200°C).
2. In a 9- × 13-inch (23 × 33 cm) enamel roasting pan, add the onion, carrots, celery, garlic, tomatoes, half of the thyme, and farro. Season with ½ teaspoon (2 mL) each salt and pepper and stir to combine. In a medium bowl, heat the broth in the micro-wave until it begins to bubble, then whisk in the tomato paste and pour over the farro and vegetables.
3. Place the chicken on a cutting board, breast side down. Using sharp kitchen shears, cut along both sides of the backbone and remove it. Discard it or reserve for making broth (page 48). Flip the chicken over, open it like a book, and press down firmly on the breastbone to flatten the bird (see Tip).
4. Pat the skin dry with paper towel. Gently slide your fingers under the skin of each breast and tuck ½ tablespoon (7 mL) butter and half of the remaining thyme leaves under each. Generously season both sides of the chicken with salt and pepper and rest it, breast side up, on the farro mixture. Sprinkle with the oregano and red pepper flakes, and dot the entire bird with the remaining 1 tablespoon (15 mL) butter.
5. Tuck the bay leaves into the farro and vegetables and roast for 55 to 60 minutes or until the chicken skin is golden brown and an instant-read thermometer inserted in the thickest part of the bird (not touching the bone) reads 165°F (75°C). You're also look-ing for the farro to be tender with a bit of a bite and for the liquid to be completely absorbed.
6. Remove the pan from the oven and let rest for 10 minutes. Remove the bay leaves and drizzle the vinegar over the farro and vegetables. (There is no need to remove the chicken when you do this. Just use a spoon and toss the farro and vegetables around the chicken to stir the vinegar into the grain and veggies.) To serve, carve the chicken or cut into whole pieces at the joints and plate with a generous serving of the farro and vegetables.

TIP: To make the spatchcocked chicken lay flat you need to break the breast bone. The easiest way to do this is to imagine you are trying to resuscitate the bird from heart failure. Also, be sure to position the legs so the chicken looks knock-kneed. The benefits of a flattened bird is that it will cook evenly with the maximum amount of coveted crispy skin.

CAJUN QUINOA WITH CHICKEN AND PEPPERS

KID FRIENDLY, QUICK COOKING, WHOLE GRAIN, GLUTEN-FREE

Serves 4 to 6

This has all the hallmarks of a family-friendly recipe—simple, healthy, and versatile—and has been enjoyed by everyone I've ever fed it to, toddlers included. I'm a big believer in exposing tiny taste buds to bold flavours (but nothing too spicy) from an early age, and I'm convinced it helps kids become better eaters. If you aren't serving this to a younger crowd, feel free to add a pinch or two of cayenne pepper to the pot along with the Cajun seasoning for an extra-spicy kick. Most commercial Cajun spice blends are heavily salted, which is why I don't salt anything in this recipe until the end. Generally, the combination of Cajun seasoning and chicken broth is enough to flavour the dish, but you can taste it before serving and decided if it needs more seasoning.

1 tablespoon (15 mL) olive oil, plus extra if needed
1 tablespoon (15 mL) butter
1½ pounds (675 g) boneless, skinless chicken breasts or thighs, cut into bite-size pieces
2 sweet bell peppers (any colour), seeded and chopped
1 medium red onion, chopped (about 1 cup/250 mL)
3 cloves garlic, grated or pressed
1 cup (250 mL) uncooked quinoa, well rinsed and drained
2 cups (500 mL) Whole Chicken Broth (page 48) or low-sodium store-bought chicken broth
1 tablespoon (15 mL) Cajun spice mix
2 tablespoons (30 mL) tomato paste
Kosher salt
Freshly ground black pepper
3 tablespoons (45 mL) chopped fresh parsley, for garnish

1. In a medium Dutch oven (4 to 6 quarts/3.8 to 5.7 L), heat the oil and butter over medium-high heat until butter is melted. Sauté the chicken until browned on both sides, about 5 minutes. You may need to do this in batches to avoid overcrowding the pan. Transfer the chicken to a plate, and add the peppers and onion to the pot. Cook until softened, adding more oil to the pan if needed and stirring frequently, about 2 to 3 minutes. Add the garlic and cook for 1 minute more.

2. Add the quinoa, broth, Cajun spice mix, and tomato paste and stir to incorporate. Bring to a boil, lower heat, and cover. Simmer for 15 minutes. Return the chicken and any accumulated juices to the pot and toss quickly to combine. Continue to cook, partially covered, until the liquid is absorbed and the quinoa is tender, 10 to 12 minutes. Turn off the heat and let rest for 10 minutes.

3. Fluff the quinoa mixture with a fork, check the seasoning, and add salt and pepper if needed. Sprinkle with parsley and serve.

TIP: Quinoa can often appear wet and mushy, even after it's been cooked. If the water isn't completely absorbed by the time the quinoa is tender, turn off the heat, drain the dish using a mesh strainer, and return it to the pot. Then, cover and let sit for 10 minutes before fluffing with a fork.

Serves 4 to 6

6 boneless, skinless chicken thighs (1 to 1½ pounds/450 to 675 g)

2 tablespoons (30 mL) olive oil, divided

1 teaspoon (5 mL) dried oregano

1½ teaspoons (7 mL) paprika

1 teaspoon (5 mL) garlic powder

1½ teaspoons (7 mL) kosher salt

½ pound (225 g) cooked chorizo, ends trimmed, sliced into ½-inch (1 cm) thick rounds

1 medium onion, diced (about 1 cup/250 mL)

1 sweet bell pepper (any colour), seeded and chopped

1½ cups (375 mL) short-grain rice (like bomba or arborio)

½ teaspoon (2 mL) ground turmeric

2 roma tomatoes, grated (about 1 cup/250 mL)

2½ cups (625 mL) Whole Chicken Broth (page 48) or low-sodium store-bought chicken broth

1 cup (250 mL) frozen peas

8 large shrimp, peeled and deveined

1 lemon, cut into wedges, for serving

TIP: You may be tempted to, but don't stir the paella. You'll be rewarded with the delicious crispy rice on the bottom of the pan, known as the socarrat.

The first time I made this dish, my teenage sons claimed it was the best thing I had put on their plates all year. Seeing as I feed a family of five three meals a day, and had spent months testing more than a hundred recipes for this book, I beamed at the high praise. Although I suggest making this in a 12-inch (30 cm) skillet, it will work in a 10-inch (25 cm) skillet as long as it's deep. For a larger group, feel free to double the recipe and cook it in a 14-inch (35 cm) pan; this recipe is forgiving and will work without issue, but to ensure that the rice cooks evenly I suggest rotating the pan on the burner frequently. Chorizo can be tricky to find, even in fine supermarkets, so here's an inspired substitution if needed: replace the paprika with smoked paprika and the chorizo with kielbasa.

1. In a large mixing bowl, combine the chicken, 1 tablespoon (15 mL) oil, oregano, paprika, garlic powder, and salt. Mix well.

2. Heat a 12-inch (30 cm) cast iron, stainless steel, or non-stick skillet over medium-high heat. Add the chicken and cook until browned, about 3 minutes per side. Transfer to a plate and set aside. Add the remaining 1 tablespoon (15 mL) oil to the skillet. Tip in the chorizo, onion, and pepper and cook until the vegetables are soft and the sausage begins to crisp, 4 to 5 minutes. Stir in the rice and turmeric, coating the rice evenly with the oil.

3. Pour the tomatoes and broth into the skillet and stir to combine. Return the chicken and any accumulated juices to the skillet. Bring to a boil, reduce the heat to medium-low, partially cover, and cook until the liquid has evaporated and the rice is tender but firm, 15 to 20 minutes.

4. Scatter in the peas and shrimp. Cover, turn off the heat, and let sit for 3 to 5 minutes, or until the shrimp are opaque and pink. Season with more salt, if needed. Garnish with lemon wedges and serve immediately.

VARIATION: Feel free to add 8 shrimp (peeled, with tails intact) and 8 mussels to the pan with the peas for a more traditional take on paella.

ROASTED SHEET PAN CHICKEN WITH POTATOES, CAULIFLOWER, AND OLIVES

Serves 4 to 6

It doesn't get any easier, or more satisfying, than serving roasted chicken and potatoes for dinner, and when the entire meal comes together on a single rimmed sheet pan, the result is comforting and ridiculously simple. The briny olives bring an unexpected burst of flavour to the recipe, and the crisp cauliflower completes the meal. If the chicken skin isn't as crisp as you crave at the end of the baking time, blast it under the broiler for a minute or two before serving.

1. Preheat the oven to 425°F (220°C). Rub a rimmed sheet pan with 1 teaspoon (5 mL) or so of the oil and set aside.
2. Pat the chicken dry with paper towel and place on the prepared sheet pan. Add the potatoes, olives, and cauliflower in a single layer surrounding the chicken.
3. Sprinkle with thyme leaves and drizzle with the remaining oil. Season with a generous pinch of salt and the red pepper flakes. Toss everything together with your hands, placing the chicken pieces skin side up and sprinkling a little extra salt on them to help the skin crisp.
4. Roast, stirring once or twice, until the chicken is cooked through and the potatoes are tender, 35 to 40 minutes.
5. Meanwhile, make the herby yogurt sauce by stirring together the yogurt, garlic, parsley, and dill. Season to taste with salt and set aside.
6. Remove the sheet pan from the oven and sprinkle the chicken and vegetables with red onion and herbs. Serve with the herby yogurt sauce and lemon wedges.

For the chicken and vegetables

¼ cup (60 mL) olive oil, divided

8 bone-in, skin-on chicken drumsticks or thighs (about 2 pounds/900 g)

1 pound (450 g) baby red potatoes, halved

½ cup (125 mL) pitted green or black olives

1 small cauliflower (about 1½ pounds/ 675 g), cut into ¾-inch (2 cm) florets

6 sprigs thyme, leaves stripped

Kosher salt

½ teaspoon (2 mL) crushed red pepper flakes

For the herby yogurt sauce

½ cup (125 mL) plain Greek yogurt

1 clove garlic, grated or pressed

¼ cup (60 mL) minced fresh parsley

¼ cup (60 mL) minced fresh dill

For serving

Thinly sliced red onions

Minced fresh herbs like parsley, mint, or both

Lemon wedges

COCONUT RICE WITH HOISIN-GLAZED TURKEY MEATBALLS

Serves 4 to 6

Coconut rice is traditionally made with jasmine rice, but during recipe testing I found that the regular long-grain kind worked best. Since it's readily available in nearly all grocery stores, that's what I went with. Sometimes reliability wins out over authenticity. It may seem strange to see sugar mixed into the rice, but I really do think it helps to elevate the flavour. The meatballs bake for a full hour with the rice, and the result is an ultra-tender bite laced with a lot of zing thanks to the garlic, ginger, and green onion. The hoisin glaze pulls everything together and becomes thick and caramelized under the broiler.

For the rice

1½ cups (375 mL) long-grain rice

1 can (14 ounces/400 mL) full-fat coconut milk

1½ cups (375 mL) Whole Chicken Broth (page 48) or low-sodium store-bought chicken broth

1 teaspoon (5 mL) sugar

1 teaspoon (5 mL) kosher salt

1 celery stalk, finely chopped

½ red pepper, finely chopped

1 carrot, peeled and finely chopped

2 cups (500 mL) frozen peas

For the meatballs

½ cup (125 mL) panko bread crumbs

¼ cup (60 mL) milk

1 large egg

2 tablespoons (30 mL) minced fresh parsley or cilantro, plus extra for garnish

2 green onions, minced, plus extra for garnish

3 cloves garlic, grated or pressed

1 teaspoon (5 mL) finely grated ginger

1 teaspoon (5 mL) soy sauce

1 teaspoon (5 mL) sesame oil

1 teaspoon (5 mL) kosher salt

1 pound (450 g) ground turkey

¼ cup (60 mL) hoisin sauce, divided

Chopped peanuts, for garnish

Sesame seeds, for garnish

1. Preheat the oven to 350°F (180°C).
2. Rinse the rice well under cold water and place in a 9- x 13-inch (23 x 33 cm) casserole dish. Add the coconut milk, broth, sugar, salt, celery, red pepper, carrot, and peas. Stir to combine and set aside.
3. In a medium mixing bowl, stir together the panko, milk, egg, parsley, green onions, garlic, ginger, soy sauce, sesame oil, and salt. Add the turkey and gently combine with a fork or your fingers, taking care not to overwork the meat.
4. Shape the meat mixture into 12 equal-size meatballs. Place on top of the rice and vegetables and, using a pastry brush, glaze the tops of the meatballs with half of the hoisin sauce.
5. Cover the casserole dish with foil and bake for 50 to 60 minutes or until the liquid has been absorbed and the rice is tender. Remove the casserole dish from the oven and let sit for 10 minutes. Turn the oven to broil.
6. Fluff the rice and vegetables with a fork, taking care not to disrupt the meatballs. Brush the meatballs with the remaining hoisin sauce and bake under the broiler for 1 to 2 minutes or until sauce is thick and caramelized. Garnish with peanuts, sesame seeds, parsley, and green onions and serve at once.

BEER-BRAISED SAUSAGES WITH CABBAGE AND POTATOES

MAKE AHEAD, KID FRIENDLY, QUICK COOKING

I make a version of this meal once a week throughout the fall and winter. I love that there's next to no prep work other than halving some potatoes and chopping an onion and a bit of cabbage. If dinner can get on the table with nothing more than a knife and cutting board, everyone from the cook to the cleanup crew is ecstatic. Although I call for bratwurst sausages in this recipe, I can assure you it works just as well with the Italian variety. If you're feeling extra fancy, serve this with a side of soft pretzels and glasses of cold beer.

2 tablespoons (30 mL) olive oil

1 pound (450 g) bratwurst sausage

1 medium red onion, sliced

½ head green cabbage, sliced

Kosher salt

Freshly ground black pepper

½ pound (225 g) new potatoes, halved

1 bottle (12 ounces/355 mL) dark beer (though any variety will work)

2 tablespoons (30 mL) Worcestershire sauce

1 tablespoon (15 mL) Dijon mustard

1½ teaspoons (7 mL) caraway seeds

2 tablespoons (30 mL) chopped fresh dill

1. In a medium Dutch oven (4 to 6 quarts/3.8 to 5.7 L), heat the oil over medium-high heat until hot and shimmering. Add the sausages and brown, turning once, about 5 minutes. Remove the sausages from the pot and transfer to a plate.

2. Stir in the onion and cabbage and season to taste with salt and pepper. Cook, stirring occasionally, until golden, about 6 minutes.

3. Return the sausages and any accumulated juices to the pot. Add the potatoes. Pour in the beer and Worcestershire sauce, stir in the mustard and caraway seeds, and bring to a boil. Reduce heat to a simmer and cook, covered, until the cabbage and potatoes are tender, about 20 minutes.

4. Uncover the pot and simmer until the liquid is almost evaporated, about 5 to 7 minutes. Check seasonings and add more salt and pepper if needed. Spoon the cabbage and potatoes onto a platter and top with sausages. Sprinkle with chopped dill and serve at once.

PERFECT SAUCY PULLED PORK

Makes 10 cups (2.5 L) pulled pork

1 cup (250 mL) ketchup

1 cup (250 mL) apple juice or pressed
   sweet apple cider

⅓ cup (85 mL) brown sugar

3 tablespoons (45 mL) Worcestershire
   sauce

2 tablespoons (30 mL) smoked paprika

2 tablespoons (30 mL) chili powder

1 teaspoon (5 mL) dry mustard powder

1 teaspoon (5 mL) hot sauce

1 boneless pork butt or shoulder (4 to
   6 pounds/1.8 to 2.7 kg), trimmed of
   excess fat

3 cloves garlic, thinly sliced

Kosher salt

Freshly ground black pepper

2 tablespoons (30 mL) olive oil

2 large onions, halved lengthwise and
   thinly sliced

TIP: 1. The meat can be cooked through step 4 up to 3 days in advance of serving. **2.** The pulled pork can be frozen in 2- to 3-cup (500 to 750 mL) portions in a freezer-safe container or zip top bag for up to 3 months.

In 1997, I moved to the south of France to work as an au pair. This is where I learned about shopping at a market and making soup from scratch. When it came to entertaining at home, I learned the most memorable tip from the family I worked for: they never made a main course on the same day they planned to serve it. Since then, this is how I approach organizing myself for a big get-together, especially during the colder months when braises and bakes are ideal make-ahead meals designed for feeding a crowd. This recipe may look long, but the steps are easy and the work is done over two or three days. I like to use boneless pork butt here, but if you can only find a piece of bone-in meat, don't discount using it. Look for something that weighs 6 to 8 pounds (2.7 to 3.6 kg), and then remove the bone from the pot when the first bake is completed.

1. Preheat the oven to 325°F (160°C). In a medium bowl or large glass measuring cup, whisk together the ketchup, apple juice, brown sugar, Worcestershire sauce, paprika, chili powder, mustard powder, and hot sauce until well combined; set aside.

2. Pat the pork dry with paper towel. Using a thin-bladed knife, make little slits all over the meat and poke a garlic slice into each hole. Generously season the pork with salt and pepper. In a large Dutch oven (7 to 9 quarts/6.6 to 8.5 L), heat the oil over medium-high heat. Brown the pork on all sides, 8 to 10 minutes total, using a pair of tongs to turn the meat as needed.

3. Transfer the seared meat to a plate and add the onions to the pot. Cook, stirring occasionally, until golden and caramelized, 5 to 7 minutes. Season with salt and pepper and stir. Return the pork to the pot, setting it on top of the onions. Pour the marinade over the meat, cover, and cook in the oven for 3 hours.

4. Remove the pot from the oven, uncover, and let cool completely. Once cool, cover the pot and set it in the refrigerator overnight.

5. Four hours before you plan on serving the pork, remove the pot from the refrigerator and skim and discard the fat from the top of the sauce. Let the meat come to room temperature for at least 2 hours. Preheat the oven to 325°F (160°C).

6. Reheat the meat for 60 to 90 minutes. By now, it should be tender and shred easily with 2 forks. Stir the shredded meat into the sauce, taste, and season with salt and pepper if needed. Serve hot.

Now that you have a pile of sweet and saucy pulled pork, what can you do with it? These are my favourite ways to serve it up:

- Make pulled pork sandwiches, of course! Pile the meat on toasted buns and top with slaw (try the Quick Cabbage Slaw on page 113).
- Make tacos by stuffing the meat into corn tortillas and topping it with chopped avocado, red cabbage, and pickled jalapeño peppers (page 248).
- Top nachos with pulled pork instead of beef.
- Stir it into macaroni and cheese (use the cheddar cheese variation on page 163).
- Make fresh spring rolls by wrapping pulled pork, fresh sliced mango, and chopped avocado with rice paper.

- Combine with cooked rice to make a pork fried rice.
- Make quesadillas by stuffing pulled pork into two flour tortillas along with pickled red onions and shredded cheese.
- Top baked russet or sweet potatoes with pulled pork, shredded Monterey Jack cheese, and green onions.
- Sauté with chopped potatoes and red peppers to make a hash. Top with a fried egg to complete the meal.

SHEET PAN SAUSAGES WITH PEPPERS AND POLENTA

Serves 4

I love to serve soft, creamy polenta topped with sausages and peppers, but doing so requires at least two cooking vessels, if not more. In an attempt to transform that crave-worthy creation into a one-pan meal, I turned to precooked polenta to help me out. The sliced polenta rounds are brushed with oil, baked until crisp on the outside and creamy within, and topped with Parmesan cheese and fresh basil. The golden polenta rounds pair perfectly with the crisp sausage, and when served with a tangle of onions, peppers, and tomatoes, the result is a quick take on classic Italian comfort food.

1. Preheat the oven to 425°F (220°C). Brush a large rimmed sheet pan with 1 tablespoon (15 mL) oil.

2. Scatter the tomatoes, onion, and peppers over the prepared sheet pan and sprinkle with oregano, basil, and red pepper flakes. Drizzle with 2 tablespoons (30 mL) oil, season with a generous pinch of salt, and toss to combine. Push the vegetables to one side of the pan.

3. Cut the polenta into 8 rounds, each approximately ½ inch (1 cm) thick. Place the sausages and polenta on the empty side of the sheet pan. Brush the tops of the polenta with the remaining 1 tablespoon (15 mL) oil and sprinkle with salt.

4. Roast until the sausages are cooked through and golden brown, 30 to 35 minutes, turning halfway through the roasting time. Remove the sheet pan from the oven, and turn the oven to broil.

5. Flip over the polenta pieces and sprinkle the rounds with the Parmesan. Return the sheet pan to the oven and broil for 3 minutes or until cheese is bubbling and the vegetables are a little blistered.

6. Sprinkle with the fresh basil and serve directly from the pan. Alternatively, place 1 or 2 polenta rounds on a plate and top with some of the vegetables and a sausage. Garnish with the fresh basil and serve at once.

4 tablespoons (60 mL) olive oil, divided

1 cup (250 mL) cherry tomatoes

1 small onion, halved and thinly sliced

2 sweet bell peppers (any colour), stemmed, seeded, and cut into ½-inch (1 cm) thick strips

½ teaspoon (2 mL) dried oregano

½ teaspoon (2 mL) dried basil

¼ teaspoon (1 mL) crushed red pepper flakes (optional)

Kosher salt

1 tube (1 pound/450 g) cooked polenta

1 pound (450 g) sweet or hot Italian sausages (chicken, turkey, or vegetarian)

½ cup (125 mL) grated Parmesan cheese

Chopped fresh basil, for serving

PORK TENDERLOIN WITH ROOT VEGETABLES AND HERBY DIPPING SAUCE

KID FRIENDLY, GLUTEN-FREE

Serves 4

½ cup (125 mL) olive oil, plus extra for pan

¼ cup (60 mL) red wine vinegar

1 tablespoon (15 mL) dried oregano

1 tablespoon (15 mL) dried basil

2 teaspoons (10 mL) dried parsley

2 teaspoons (10 mL) kosher salt

1 teaspoon (5 mL) freshly ground black pepper

1 teaspoon (5 mL) smoked paprika

1 teaspoon (5 mL) garlic powder

¼ teaspoon (1 mL) crushed red pepper flakes

3 parsnips (about ¾ pound/340 g), peeled and cut into 2-inch (5 cm) pieces, halving them if large

2 sweet potatoes (about ¾ pound/340 g), peeled, halved, and cut into ½-inch (1 cm) thick pieces

1 pork tenderloin (about 1½ pounds/675 g), trimmed (see Tip)

¼ cup (60 mL) mayonnaise

4 cups (1 L) baby spinach or other tender leafy green

TIP: Tenderloins have an area of connective tissue known as silver skin. Silverwhite in colour, it's the thick membrane that runs along the side of the tenderloin. It needs to be trimmed away, as it won't break down during cooking, instead becoming chewy and stringy. To trim, slide the tip of a knife under the silver skin, tilt the knife upward, and remove thin pieces of skin until it's completely gone. Be careful not to confuse fat with silver skin: if you can pull it off, it's fat; if you can't, you know it's silver skin.

If it isn't already, pork tenderloin needs to be on your radar. Affordable, flavourful, and quick cooking, it's also lean and incredibly versatile, and it pairs well with most produce. Have I convinced you yet? I used to sear my pork in a skillet before popping it into the oven to finish, but I find that it cooks more evenly when I roast it in the oven. You want to be careful not to overcook your pork tenderloin, otherwise you'll lose the juiciness and tenderness this cut of meat is known for. If parsnips are unavailable, feel free to use carrots instead.

1. Preheat the oven to 425°F (220°C). Rub a rimmed sheet pan with a small amount of olive oil and set aside.

2. In a large bowl, whisk together the oil, vinegar, oregano, basil, parsley, salt, pepper, paprika, garlic powder, and red pepper flakes. Remove 2 tablespoons (30 mL) of the marinade and set aside.

3. Add the parsnips, sweet potatoes, and pork tenderloin to the marinade and toss to combine. Cover the bowl with plastic wrap and refrigerate for 30 minutes.

4. Using tongs, transfer the pork tenderloin to the centre of the prepared pan and scatter the vegetables around the meat. Bake for 30 to 35 minutes or until the pork is cooked through. An instant-read thermometer inserted into the centre of the pork should read 145°F (65°C). Place the cooked pork on a plate, cover with aluminum foil, and let rest for 10 minutes. Return the sheet pan to the oven and roast the vegetables for another 10 minutes. They should be tender and golden brown at this point.

5. While the pork and vegetables are cooking, make the dipping sauce by whisking the reserved marinade with the mayonnaise. Chill until ready to serve.

6. Scatter the spinach over the vegetables on the sheet pan and toss to combine. The residual heat will help to wilt the greens. Thinly slice the pork and add it back to the sheet pan. Serve immediately with the dipping sauce.

BAKED BEEF KOFTA WITH COUSCOUS

Serves 6 to 8

Made with ground meat and spices, a beef kofta is the Mediterranean cousin of the classic meatball. Oblong in shape, and usually skewered and barbecued, my version is baked in the oven on a wire rack under high heat.

1. To make the beef kofta mixture, using the largest holes on a box grater, grate the onion into a medium mixing bowl. You should have about ¼ cup (60 mL). Stir in the garlic, ginger, parsley, and mint. Crumble the ground beef over the aromatics and sprinkle with the salt, coriander, cumin, oregano, cinnamon, cloves, and red pepper flakes. Mix quickly with your hands, taking care not to overwork the meat, otherwise it will end up tough. Cover the bowl with plastic wrap and place in the refrigerator for at least 3 hours. You can also prepare the meat mixture a day in advance and refrigerate until needed.

2. To make the yogurt sauce, place the yogurt, mint, garlic, and lemon zest and juice in a mason jar and season to taste with salt. Shake to combine. Store in the refrigerator for 1 hour or up to 2 days.

3. When you're ready to bake the kofta, preheat the oven to 450°F (230°C). Line a rimmed sheet pan with aluminum foil. Place a wire rack over top and lightly mist with olive oil or non-stick cooking spray. Shape ½ cup (125 mL) beef mixture into an oblong meatball and place it on the prepared rack. Repeat with the remaining meat until you have 12 meatballs in total. Bake for 15 to 18 minutes or until cooked through. Turn the oven to broil, and cook for an additional 3 to 4 minutes or until the meat is lightly crisp and charred.

4. While the beef is baking, make the couscous. Place the couscous in a bowl that is large enough for it to double in volume. Add ½ teaspoon (2 mL) salt and the butter. Bring 1½ cups (375 mL) of water to a boil in a kettle and pour into the bowl with the couscous. Stir, and then cover the bowl with a plate or plastic wrap and let stand for 8 to 10 minutes or until all the liquid is absorbed. Whisk together the oil, lemon zest, 2 tablespoons (30 mL) lemon juice, and the remaining ½ teaspoon (2 mL) salt. Remove the cover from the bowl and fluff the couscous with a fork. Pour the olive oil mixture over top, add the parsley and shallot, and stir well to combine. Taste and adjust seasoning, adding more lemon juice and salt if needed.

5. To serve, spoon the couscous onto plates and top a few pieces of beef kofta with a dollop of yogurt sauce.

For the beef kofta
½ large Spanish onion
2 cloves garlic, grated or pressed
1 tablespoon (15 mL) grated ginger
¼ cup (60 mL) chopped fresh parsley
2 tablespoons (30 mL) chopped fresh mint
2 pounds (900 g) medium ground beef
2 teaspoons (10 mL) kosher salt
1 tablespoon (15 mL) ground coriander
1 tablespoon (15 mL) ground cumin
1 teaspoon (5 mL) dried oregano
½ teaspoon (2 mL) ground cinnamon
¼ teaspoon (1 mL) ground cloves
Pinch of crushed red pepper flakes

For the yogurt sauce
1 cup (250 mL) plain Greek yogurt
    (or ½ cup/125 mL plain yogurt +
    ½ cup/125 mL sour cream)
¼ cup (60 mL) finely chopped mint
½ clove garlic, grated or pressed
Zest and juice of 1 small lemon
Kosher salt

For the couscous
1½ cups (375 mL) couscous
1 teaspoon (5 mL) kosher salt, divided
1 tablespoon (15 mL) butter
2 tablespoons (30 mL) olive oil
Zest and juice of 1 small lemon
½ cup (125 mL) fresh parsley, roughly chopped
1 shallot, minced

TIP: I like to serve this dish with fresh, sliced tomatoes, cucumbers, and onion drizzled with olive oil and a small splash of red wine vinegar. As always, season to taste with salt and pepper, and if you're feeling fancy, add a pinch of dried oregano on top.

ONE-POT BAKED BEEFARONI

Serves 6 to 8

2 small onions, peeled and quartered

2 large carrots, peeled and cut into
   3-inch (8 cm) pieces

2 celery stalks, cut into 3-inch (8 cm)
   pieces

4 cloves garlic

1 tablespoon (15 mL) olive oil

1 tablespoon (15 mL) dried oregano

1 teaspoon (5 mL) crushed red pepper
   flakes

1 teaspoon (5 mL) salt

1 pound (450 g) medium ground beef

3 cups (750 mL) Whole Chicken Broth
   (page 48) or low-sodium store-
   bought chicken broth

½ cup (125 mL) red wine

1 can (28 ounces/796 mL) crushed
   tomatoes

2 tablespoons (30 mL) Worcestershire
   sauce

2 tablespoons (30 mL) tomato paste

¼ cup (60 mL) packed fresh basil
   leaves, stems removed and chopped

1 pound (450 g) macaroni pasta

1 cup (250 mL) grated mozzarella
   cheese

½ cup (125 mL) grated Parmesan
   cheese

Minced fresh parsley, for serving
   (optional)

Around the time my older boys became teenagers, my husband and I noticed that they wanted to spend most of their free time on the weekends with their friends. I started to dislike having our family divided up at the end of the weekend, and we quickly launched what we affectionately refer to as Family Supper Sundays. The goal is to share a casual meal with our kids and extended family every Sunday. If you don't have a big family, I still encourage you to gather those you consider dearest around your table as often as possible; I guarantee only good things will come of it. Otherwise, I wouldn't be willing to feed up to twenty-three people every Sunday. Oh, and when you have all of those amazing people around your table, serve them this one-pot twist on everyone's favourite family-night meal: pasta with meat sauce.

1. Place the onions, carrots, celery, and garlic in the bowl of a food processor fitted with a steel blade. Pulse until finely chopped. Remove the cover and scrape down the sides of the bowl with a rubber spatula. Return the cover and pulse 4 to 5 more times.

2. Preheat the oven to 350°F (180°C). In a large Dutch oven (7 to 9 quarts/6.6 to 8.5 L), heat the oil over medium heat. Add the vegetable mixture and cook, stirring frequently, until softened, 3 to 4 minutes. Stir in the oregano, red pepper flakes, and salt and cook 1 minute more.

3. Crumble the beef into the pot and cook, stirring occasionally, for 5 minutes or until meat is browned. Stir in the broth, wine, tomatoes, Worcestershire sauce, tomato paste, basil, and pasta. Bring to a boil, lower the heat to medium, and cook, stirring frequently, for 11 to 13 minutes or until the pasta is nearly cooked but firm to the bite.

4. Sprinkle the mozzarella and Parmesan over the pasta. Bake the beefaroni for 10 minutes or until the cheeses are melted and the pasta is cooked through. Remove the pot from the oven and let stand for 10 minutes. Sprinkle with the parsley, if using, and serve.

SLOW-COOKED PULLED BEEF AND BAKED POTATO "POUTINE"

Serves 4 to 6

MAKE AHEAD, KID FRIENDLY

For the pulled beef

1 cup (250 mL) beef broth

¼ cup (60 mL) steak sauce

¼ cup (60 mL) Worcestershire sauce

3 pounds (1.4 kg) pot roast, such as
    blade or brisket

Kosher salt

Freshly ground black pepper

2 tablespoons (30 mL) olive oil

1 onion, cut lengthwise into quarters

3 cloves garlic, thinly sliced

For the potatoes

4 large russet potatoes

2 teaspoons (10 mL) olive oil

Kosher salt

For serving

1 cup (250 mL) white cheddar cheese
    curds

3 green onions, thinly sliced

Chopped fresh parsley

Sour cream (optional)

This super-simple crowd-pleasing recipe uses basic pantry ingredients that come together in a snap, leaving you free to play all day as dinner simmers in the oven. If you aren't up to making the poutine part of the recipe, serve the pulled beef on buns, smear it over pizza, or toss it with some cooked rice. Then, fill your freezer with any leftovers for future dinners or lunches.

1. Preheat the oven to 325°F (160°C). In a medium bowl or large glass measuring cup, whisk together the beef broth, steak sauce, and Worcestershire sauce until well combined; set aside.

2. Pat the beef dry with paper towel and generously season with salt and pepper. In a medium Dutch oven (4 to 6 quarts/3.8 to 5.7 L), heat the oil over medium-high heat. Brown the beef on all sides, 8 to 10 minutes total, using a pair of tongs to turn the meat as needed.

3. Transfer the seared meat to a plate and add the onions and garlic to the pot. Season with salt and pepper. Cook, stirring occasionally, until golden and caramelized, 5 to 7 minutes. Return the beef to the pot, setting it on top of the onions and garlic. Pour the broth mixture over the meat, cover, and transfer to the oven. Cook for 3½ to 4 hours or until the meat is tender and can be shredded easily.

4. Meanwhile, rub the potatoes with the oil, sprinkle with salt, and wrap each potato tightly in aluminum foil. Prick with the tines of a fork. After the beef has been in the oven for 2 hours, place the wrapped potatoes directly on the oven rack beside the pot and bake for the remaining time, 1½ to 2 hours.

5. Remove the pot and potatoes from the oven and set aside the potatoes. Transfer the beef to a plate and remove any twine that may be holding the meat together. Using 2 forks, pull the roast into shreds. Set the pot over medium-high heat and bring the liquid to a boil. Lower the temperature to medium and simmer until the liquid is reduced by half. Return the pulled beef to the pot and toss with the liquid to combine.

6. To assemble the poutine, place a potato on each plate and cut open. Top with pulled beef and cheese curds and drizzle with some of the sauce in the pot. Garnish with green onions and parsley and top with a dollop of sour cream, if using.

CIDER-BRAISED MUSSELS WITH MUSTARD AND CREAM

Serves 4

Mussels are real fast food. They also happen to be incredibly inexpensive compared to other types of seafood, making them ideal for when you're looking for something special to serve to guests. While many recipes instruct cooks to clean and debeard the mussels, most commercially bought mussels will already be cleaned of their threads. To prep the mussels for cooking, a quick rinse in a colander is all that's required. Don't forget: live mussels should be closed tightly, so be sure to discard any that are open before cooking.

1. Rinse the mussels in a colander and check them, as they should be tightly closed. If you discover an open shell, tap it lightly against the counter. If the mussel is alive, the shell should close. If it doesn't, then discard it.
2. In a medium Dutch oven (4 to 6 quarts/3.8 to 5.7 L), heat the oil and butter over medium heat. Add the shallots and garlic to the pot and cook, stirring often, for 3 to 4 minutes or until the shallots are soft and fragrant. Sprinkle with thyme and whisk in the mustard. Pour in the cider and increase the heat to medium-high.
3. Add the mussels to the pot, stir with a wooden spoon, cover, and steam the mussels until they open, shaking the pot once or twice during cooking, about 5 minutes. Remove the lid and check the mussels. If all of them aren't open, cover and cook for another 1 to 2 minutes. Discard any mussels that haven't opened after this time.
4. Using a slotted spoon, transfer the mussels to a large bowl. Increase the heat to high and boil the liquid for 3 minutes or until it reduces by a third. Stir in the lemon juice and season to taste with salt and pepper. Reduce the heat to low and whisk in the crème fraîche. Return the mussels to the pot and toss to coat with the cream sauce, stirring until the mussels are warmed through.
5. To serve, divide the mussels between 4 bowls and spoon some of the sauce over top. Garnish with parsley and lemon wedges and serve with the baguette to mop up the sauce.

4 pounds (1.8 kg) mussels, cleaned and debearded if necessary

1 tablespoon (15 mL) olive oil

1 tablespoon (15 mL) butter

2 shallots, minced

3 cloves garlic, grated or pressed

2 sprigs thyme, leaves stripped

1 tablespoon (15 mL) grainy Dijon mustard

1 bottle (12 ounces/355 mL) preferred hard cider

1 tablespoon (15 mL) fresh lemon juice

Kosher salt

Freshly ground black pepper

¼ cup (60 mL) crème fraîche

Parsley, for garnish

Lemon wedges, for garnish

Crusty baguette, for serving

Serves 4

For the salmon and veggies

1 pound (450 g) baby potatoes, halved

3 tablespoons (45 mL) olive oil, divided

Kosher salt

¾ pound (340 g) fresh asparagus, ends trimmed

Zest of 1 lime

4 skin-on salmon filets (4 to 5 ounces/ 110 to 140 g each)

2 tablespoons (30 mL) light brown sugar

1 tablespoon (15 mL) chili powder

Pinch of cayenne pepper

For the avocado cream sauce

1 medium ripe avocado, peeled and pitted

2 tablespoons (30 mL) fresh lime juice

3 tablespoons (45 mL) sour cream

2 tablespoons (30 mL) chopped fresh cilantro or parsley, plus extra for garnish

1 clove garlic

½ teaspoon (2 mL) kosher salt

BROWN SUGAR AND CHILI–RUBBED SALMON SHEET PAN DINNER

KID FRIENDLY, QUICK COOKING, GLUTEN-FREE

It's hard to overstate just how much I love this casual and quick-cooking weeknight meal. Heart-healthy slices of salmon are sprinkled with a sweet and spicy dry rub and roasted to melt-in-your-mouth perfection. The potatoes, slick with olive oil and salt, take a turn in the oven first, to develop the golden brown and crispy exterior we covet, before meeting up with asparagus and salmon for a final roasting session. Dollops of avocado cream sauce complete the dish and provide a cool complement to the zippy salmon.

1. Preheat the oven to 425°F (220°C). Line a rimmed sheet pan with parchment paper or aluminum foil.
2. Scatter the potatoes over the prepared pan and drizzle with 1 tablespoon (15 mL) oil. Sprinkle with salt and toss to combine. Place the potatoes cut side down and roast for 10 minutes or until the potatoes begin to brown on the bottom.
3. Turn the potatoes and push to one side of the pan. Add the asparagus to the empty side. Drizzle with 1 tablespoon (15 mL) oil and sprinkle with the lime zest. Season to taste with salt. Using tongs (because the pan is hot), carefully toss the asparagus to combine and then push to the edges of the pan, leaving space in the middle for the salmon filets.
4. Place the salmon filets, skin side down, in the middle of the sheet pan and brush with the remaining 1 tablespoon (15 mL) oil. In a small bowl, combine the brown sugar, chili powder, ½ teaspoon (2 mL) salt, and cayenne. Sprinkle the brown sugar mixture evenly over each filet, rubbing it into the tops of the filets.
5. Roast for 10 to 12 minutes or until the salmon is just cooked through and the asparagus is still crisp.
6. Meanwhile, make the avocado cream sauce. In the bowl of a food processor fitted with a steel blade, combine the avocado, lime juice, sour cream, cilantro, garlic, and salt. Blend until smooth.
7. To serve, divide the potatoes and asparagus between 4 plates. Top each with a piece of salmon and a dollop of the avocado cream sauce. Garnish with the cilantro and serve.

STOVETOP SHRIMP BOIL

Serves 6 to 8

You may not hear the rush of waves, but you're certain to hear hurrying feet as everyone clamours to the table for this eat-with-your-fingers feast that's a party on the plate. Chopped potatoes, corn on the cob, cured sausage, and seasoned shrimp combine to make a mainland meal that rivals any coastal concoction.

1. In a large Dutch oven (7 to 9 quarts/6.6 to 8.5 L), combine the water and beer. Add ½ cup (125 mL) Old Bay seasoning, salt, garlic, onion, thyme, and bay leaves. Squeeze the juice from the lemon into the liquid and toss in the lemon halves. Bring the water to a boil, cover, reduce heat to medium-low, and cook for 5 minutes.

2. Add the potatoes to the pot, cover, and cook for 8 minutes or until tender. Add the corn and cook for another 5 minutes. Toss the sausage and shrimp into the pot, cover, and cook until the shrimp are opaque and cooked through, 3 to 4 minutes.

3. Using a slotted spoon, transfer the sausage, shrimp, and vegetables to a large bowl or tray. Sprinkle with the remaining 2 tablespoons (30 mL) Old Bay seasoning.

4. Ladle 1 cup (250 mL) of the cooking liquid (no solid pieces) into a bowl. Add the butter and stir until the butter is melted. Cover a table with several layers of newspaper and serve the shrimp boil with the buttery sauce, lemon wedges, and hunks of baguette.

4 cups (1 L) water

1 bottle (12 ounces/355 mL) beer, any variety

½ cup + 2 tablespoons (155 mL) Old Bay seasoning (or your favourite shrimp or seafood spice blend)

2 tablespoons (30 mL) kosher salt

4 cloves garlic, peeled and smashed

1 onion, unpeeled and quartered

4 sprigs thyme

2 bay leaves

1 lemon, scrubbed and halved, plus extra wedges for serving

1½ pounds (675 g) new red potatoes, quartered

4 ears corn, husked and halved

1 pound (450 g) chorizo or kielbasa sausage, cut into ½-inch (1 cm) cubes

1 pound (450 g) shrimp, deveined and shell on

3 tablespoons (45 mL) unsalted butter

1 fresh baguette, for serving

CHILI-LIME POTATO NACHOS

VEGETARIAN, KID FRIENDLY, QUICK COOKING,
GLUTEN-FREE

Serves 4

Despite looking like something Jackson Pollock may have painted, this colourful sheet pan supper is a real crowd-pleaser and works just as well for Game Day as it does for Wednesday night dinner. Chili, lime, and paprika act as the flavour base for the potatoes, and when roasted at high heat the surface of the potato wedges become golden brown and crispy, reminiscent of the missing nacho chips. The beans add a protein punch and the melted cheese makes it feel like a real treat. Top with salsa, sour cream, and chopped avocado for an authentic-tasting dish.

1. Preheat the oven to 425°F (220°C).
2. In a medium mixing bowl, whisk together the oil, egg white, chili powder, cumin, garlic powder, paprika, oregano, salt, and lime juice until completely combined.
3. Add the potato wedges to the mixing bowl and toss, coating them evenly in the oil and spice mixture. Spread the potatoes in a single layer on a rimmed sheet pan and bake for 30 to 35 minutes, flipping once, or until golden brown with a crispy exterior.
4. Remove the sheet pan from the oven and sprinkle potatoes with the beans, tomatoes, and cheese. Return to the oven and bake for another 5 minutes or until the cheese is melted. Garnish with the salsa, sour cream, avocado, and green onion and serve hot directly on the sheet pan, with cilantro, jalapeños and lime wedges, if using.

2 tablespoons (30 mL) olive oil

1 large egg white

½ teaspoon (2 mL) chili powder

½ teaspoon (2 mL) ground cumin

¼ teaspoon (1 mL) garlic powder

¼ teaspoon (1 mL) smoked paprika

¼ teaspoon (1 mL) dried oregano

1 teaspoon (5 mL) kosher salt

1½ teaspoons (7 mL) lime juice

4 large russet potatoes, scrubbed clean and sliced into thick wedges

1 can (19 ounces/540 mL) black or pinto beans, drained and rinsed

½ cup (125 mL) cherry tomatoes, halved

2 cups (500 mL) shredded cheddar or Monterey Jack cheese (or a mixture of both)

½ cup (125 mL) prepared salsa

½ cup (125 mL) sour cream, crème fraîche, or plain Greek yogurt

1 avocado, peeled, pitted, and diced

2 green onions, trimmed and thinly sliced

Optional toppings for serving: fresh cilantro, pickled jalapeños, lime wedges

CRISPY BLACK BEAN TACOS

VEGETARIAN, KID FRIENDLY, QUICK COOKING,
GLUTEN-FREE

Serves 2 to 4

1 can (19 ounces/540 mL) black beans,
   drained and rinsed
½ cup (125 mL) minced red onion
2 cloves garlic, grated or pressed
2 tablespoons (30 mL) minced fresh
   cilantro
1 tablespoon (15 mL) fresh lime juice
1 teaspoon (5 mL) chili powder
½ teaspoon (2 mL) ground cumin
Kosher salt
2 tablespoons (30 mL) olive oil
8 white or yellow corn tortillas
1 cup (250 mL) grated Monterey Jack
   cheese or crumbled feta cheese
Optional toppings for serving: chopped
   fresh cilantro, sour cream

With this cross between a hard-shell taco and a quesadilla, you'll have a hard time eating tacos any other way once you give this pan-fried crispy version a try. Feel free to get creative with the fillings by changing the type of bean (pinto beans are also great) or substituting leftover chicken or steak. These also make a popular party snack, especially when sliced in half and served with bowls of salsa and guacamole for dipping.

1. Preheat the oven to 250°F (120°C) and place a piece of parchment paper inside the oven on the middle rack.
2. In a medium bowl, combine the beans, onion, garlic, cilantro, lime juice, chili powder, cumin, and a generous pinch of salt. Lightly mash the ingredients together with the back of a fork or a pastry cutter, which makes quick work of the task.
3. Set a medium cast iron, stainless steel, or non-stick skillet over medium-high heat. Add a drizzle of oil and place a corn tortilla in the pan. Let it get hot in the oil for a few seconds to make it pliable, and then spoon ¼ cup (60 mL) of the bean filling over half of the tortilla and top with a sprinkling of cheese. Try not to overfill the tacos, otherwise you might lose some of the filling when you flip them.
4. Using a spatula, carefully fold over the empty half of the tortilla to form a pocket. Press down lightly on the tortilla so it holds its shape. As this first taco cooks, move it to the side of the pan and begin a second one using the steps outlined above. Depending on the size of your pan, you can cook 2 or 3 tacos at once.
5. Cook each taco until browned and crispy, about 3 minutes per side. When flipping the taco to cook on the other side, use a spatula and flip the taco toward the fold so the filling doesn't fall out. If your pan is dry between batches, add more oil.
6. Place the cooked tacos in the warm oven on the parchment paper while you finish cooking the rest of the tacos. If the tacos are very greasy, blot them with a paper towel before moving them to the oven. Serve tacos with cilantro and sour cream, if using.

SAMOSA SKILLET POT PIE WITH MINTED YOGURT SAUCE

Serves 4 to 6

This pot pie sees a lot of table time in my home in the fall and winter. The flavours are mild, making it a great way to introduce Indian cuisine to family members who may be apprehensive about new spices. Fortunately, it's also exciting enough to impress any special guests you invite for dinner. I like to serve this with a simple green salad to offset the heavy pastry and potato combo.

1. Preheat the oven to 425°F (220°C). In an oven-safe 10-inch (25 cm) cast iron or stainless steel skillet, heat 2 tablespoons (30 mL) oil over medium heat. Add the cumin and fennel seeds; when the seeds begin to sizzle, add the onion and cook for 5 minutes or until soft and translucent.

2. Stir in the ginger, turmeric, cumin, garam masala, salt, pepper, and cayenne and cook for 1 minute more. Add the potatoes, and additional oil if the pan is looking dry, and cook for 5 minutes, stirring occasionally, or until the outer edges begin to crisp and turn golden brown. Add the broth; bring to a boil, reduce the heat, and simmer, partially covered, for 20 to 25 minutes or until the potatoes are tender and the liquid is thick and saucy. Stir every few minutes to keep the potatoes from sticking to the bottom of the skillet.

3. Add the peas and cilantro, and cook for 1 minute more. Taste and adjust the seasonings if needed. Remove the skillet from the heat.

4. Lightly flour a work surface and roll the puff pastry into a 12-inch (30 cm) square. Cover the skillet with the pastry, tucking the edges in and around the vegetable mixture. To make an egg wash, lightly beat together the egg and water. Brush the top of the pastry with the egg wash and cut 4 small slits in the centre for steam to escape.

5. Bake the pie for 15 to 20 minutes or until the crust is beginning to brown. Reduce the heat to 375°F (190°C) and bake until the pastry is golden brown and crisp, 10 to 20 minutes. Remove the skillet from the oven and let rest for 10 minutes before cutting.

6. While the pie is baking, make the minted yogurt sauce. In a small bowl, combine the yogurt, mint, garlic, lemon juice, cumin, and cayenne. Season to taste with salt and pepper. Let sit for 30 minutes.

7. Serve the pie with the minted yogurt sauce and mango chutney, and garnish with cilantro, if using. Store any leftover sauce in the refrigerator for up to 5 days.

For the pot pie

2 to 3 tablespoons (10 to 15 mL) coconut oil

1 teaspoon (5 mL) cumin seeds

½ teaspoon (2 mL) fennel seeds

1 medium onion, finely chopped

1 tablespoon (15 mL) grated, peeled fresh ginger

1 teaspoon (5 mL) ground turmeric

1 teaspoon (5 mL) ground cumin

½ teaspoon (2 mL) garam masala

1 teaspoon (5 mL) kosher salt

½ teaspoon (2 mL) freshly ground black pepper

Pinch of cayenne pepper

2 cups (500 mL) diced, unpeeled Yukon Gold potatoes

1½ cups (375 mL) vegetable broth

1 cup (250 mL) frozen peas

2 tablespoons (30 mL) chopped fresh cilantro

1 sheet puff pastry, thawed

1 large egg

1 tablespoon (15 mL) water

For the sauce

1 cup (250 mL) plain Greek yogurt

½ cup (125 mL) finely chopped fresh mint

2 medium cloves garlic, grated or pressed

1 tablespoon (15 mL) fresh lemon juice

½ teaspoon (2 mL) cumin

Pinch of cayenne pepper

Kosher salt

Freshly ground black pepper

Optional toppings for serving: mango chutney, chopped fresh cilantro

SKILLET GNOCCHI WITH BACON AND PEAS

KID FRIENDLY, QUICK COOKING

½ cup (125 mL) Whole Chicken Broth (page 48) or low-sodium store-bought chicken broth

½ cup (125 mL) milk

2 teaspoons (10 mL) all-purpose flour

6 strips thick-cut bacon, chopped

1 package (2 pounds/1 kg) prepared gnocchi

2 cups (500 mL) frozen peas, thawed

1 cup (250 mL) grated mozzarella cheese

½ cup (125 mL) grated Parmesan cheese

1 tablespoon (15 mL) chopped fresh basil

Perfect for feeding a crowd or a group of hungry teenagers, this dish is made with pantry and fridge staples that I almost always have on hand. I like to round out the meal with a large green salad and have even been known to set this on the table and let my kids devour it straight from the pan.

1. Position a rack in the top third of the oven and preheat to broil. In a glass measuring cup, whisk together the broth, milk, and flour; set aside.

2. Cook the bacon in a 12-inch (30 cm) oven-safe cast iron, stainless steel, or non-stick skillet over high heat, stirring as needed until crisp, about 6 minutes. Transfer to a plate lined with paper towel and drain all but 1 tablespoon (15 mL) of bacon fat from the skillet.

3. Add the gnocchi to the skillet and reduce the heat to medium. Cook for 7 minutes or until the gnocchi is lightly browned and tender, stirring frequently to prevent it from sticking to the bottom of the pan. If some bits do stick, don't worry about it. You can scrape them up with a spatula once the liquid is added to the pan.

4. Return the bacon to the skillet and add the peas. Cook for 1 minute, stirring all the while. Pour the milk mixture into the skillet and stir, cooking for 1 minute more. Sprinkle the gnocchi with the mozzarella and Parmesan. Transfer the skillet to the oven and broil for 2 to 3 minutes or until the cheeses are melted and lightly browned. Sprinkle with the basil and serve at once.

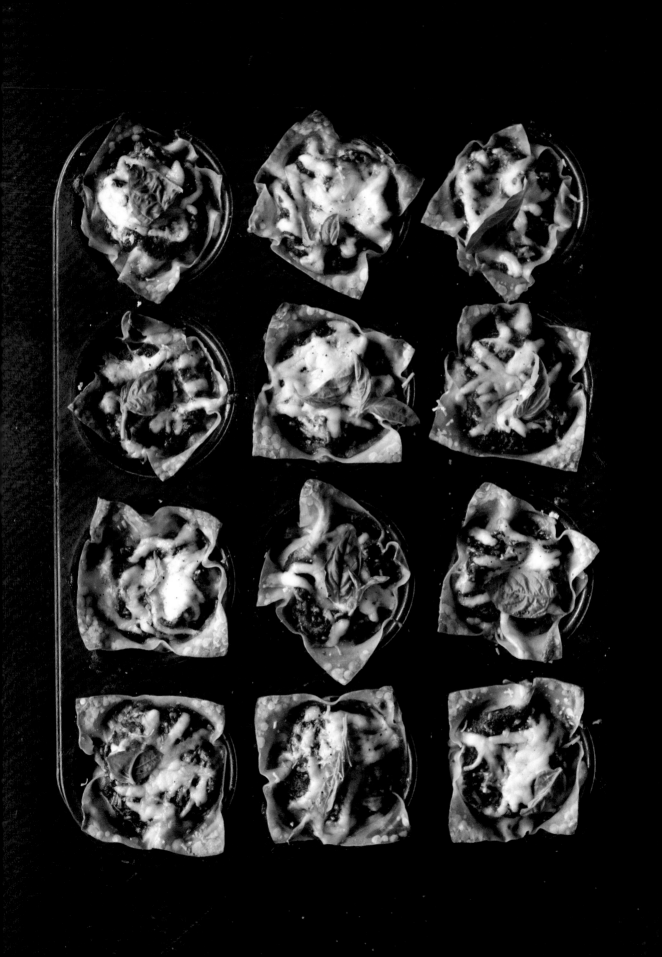

SPINACH AND RICOTTA WONTON MINI LASAGNAS

VEGETARIAN, MAKE AHEAD, KID FRIENDLY, QUICK COOKING

This is probably the easiest lasagna you will ever make. The convenient single-serving size is perfect for small stomachs, packed lunches, picnics, or just calorie-counting eaters in search of something properly portioned. Wonton wrappers can be found in the refrigerated section of the produce aisle (where you would find soups, salad dressings, and containers of baby spinach or mixed greens). They are typically sold in packs of fifty-six and you can freeze what you don't use, saving them for a second supper.

1. Preheat the oven to 375°F (190°C). Lightly oil a standard 12-cup muffin tin, or coat with non-stick spray.
2. In a medium bowl, combine the ricotta, spinach, ½ cup (125 mL) Parmesan, garlic, egg, salt, and pepper and stir to blend.
3. Press 1 wonton wrapper into each of the muffin cups. Divide the ricotta mixture evenly between the 12 wonton wrappers and top with 1 tablespoon (15 mL) each of tomato sauce and mozzarella. Top with another wonton wrapper layer and another tablespoon (15 mL) each of tomato sauce and mozzarella. Sprinkle with the remaining ¼ cup (60 mL) Parmesan, dividing it evenly between the cups.
4. Bake for 15 to 17 minutes or until the cheese has melted and the wonton wrappers are crisp and golden brown. Remove the muffin tin from the oven and let cool for 5 minutes. Garnish with basil, if using, before serving.

TIP: This recipe can be made through step 3 and then covered and frozen for up to 1 month. To bake from frozen, follow step 4, adding a few extra minutes to the cooking time if needed.

Serves 4 to 6; makes 12 mini lasagnas

1 cup (250 mL) whole milk ricotta cheese

1 cup (250 mL) packed baby spinach, finely chopped

¾ cup (175 mL) grated Parmesan cheese, divided

1 garlic clove, grated or pressed

1 large egg, beaten

¾ teaspoon (4 mL) kosher salt

½ teaspoon (2 mL) freshly ground black pepper

24 wonton wrappers

1½ cups (375 mL) Roasted Tomato Sauce (page 244) or your favourite store-bought tomato sauce

1½ cups (375 mL) grated mozzarella cheese

Fresh basil leaves, for garnish (optional)

Serves 4

¼ cup (60 mL) extra-virgin olive oil,
    plus extra to finish
1 medium yellow onion, grated
1 clove garlic, grated or pressed
Kosher salt
1 cup (250 mL) pot barley
4 cups (1 L) Whole Chicken Broth
    (page 48) or store-bought chicken
    or vegetable broth
2 medium zucchini, finely diced
½ pint cherry tomatoes, halved (about
    1 cup/250 mL)
¾ cup (175 mL) parsley leaves,
    chopped
¾ cup (175 mL) basil leaves, finely
    chopped
Freshly ground black pepper
¼ cup (60 mL) freshly grated Parmesan
    cheese, plus extra for garnish

LATE SUMMER BARLEY RISOTTO

MAKE AHEAD, KID FRIENDLY, GLUTEN-FREE

They say what grows together goes together, so why not take full advantage of late summer's succulent produce to make a meatless meal that's designed for warm-weather eating. Like rice, barley is high in starch and lends itself well to being simmered and stirred into a creamy risotto, but the high fibre content will help keep you feeling full for just a little longer. Feel free to stir fresh corn into the pot as well, and if you're feeling extra daring you can start the dish with a few strips of bacon (skip the oil and use the bacon fat to sauté the onion and garlic). To make the dish vegan, use vegetable broth and omit the Parmesan cheese at the end.

1. In a medium Dutch oven (4 to 6 quarts/3.8 to 5.7 L), heat the oil over medium-high heat. Add the onion and garlic, season with a generous pinch of salt, and sauté until softened, about 3 minutes.
2. Stir in the barley, broth, and zucchini and bring to a boil. Reduce the heat, cover, and simmer for 45 minutes, stirring vigorously for 15 seconds or so once or twice through the cooking time.
3. Fold in the tomatoes, parsley, basil, pepper, and Parmesan. Taste and check seasonings, adding more salt if needed. Serve with a drizzle of oil and additional Parmesan.

HORSERADISH AND HAVARTI MACARONI AND CHEESE

Serves 4 to 6

What's better than a bowl of macaroni and cheese? How about one that's been spiked with horseradish and Havarti and cooked in a single pot? Stovetop versions of this classic meal abound, but I like baking mine in the oven instead. I find that the pasta develops a better bite, and although the cook time is a little longer, it's mostly hands-off, freeing you up to do other things. Be sure to use the best quality cheese available, since you'll be including plenty of it.

1. Preheat the oven to 375°F (190°C).
2. In a medium Dutch oven (4 to 6 quarts/3.8 to 5.7 L), whisk together the milk, water, evaporated milk, horseradish, salt, Dijon, and pepper over medium heat. Bring to a boil, then quickly and carefully stir in the pasta.
3. Transfer the pot to the oven and bake for 15 to 20 minutes, stirring halfway through, or until the noodles are al dente and almost all of the liquid has been absorbed. The mixture will look curdled, but don't fret—that's how it's supposed to look. It all comes together as a smooth sauce in the end.
4. Remove the pot from the oven and add the butter and Havarti, a few handfuls at a time, stirring until completely melted. The sauce will thicken as the cheese melts, and the pasta will become more tender. If you prefer a creamier pasta, stir in more milk, 1 to 2 tablespoons (15 to 30 mL) at a time, until the cheese sauce reaches the desired consistency. Taste and adjust seasonings, adding more salt if needed. Sprinkle with chives or dill, if using.

VARIATION: To turn this dish into a classic, more kid-friendly macaroni and cheese, eliminate the horseradish and use grated aged cheddar cheese (or a mix of cheddar and Gruyère) in place of the Havarti.

2 cups (500 mL) 2% milk, plus extra for finishing

1 cup (250 mL) water

1 can (12 ounces/354 mL) evaporated milk

2 tablespoons (30 mL) horseradish

2 teaspoons (10 mL) kosher salt

1 tablespoon (15 mL) Dijon mustard

½ teaspoon (2 mL) freshly ground black pepper

1 pound (450 g) macaroni or small shells pasta

2 tablespoons (30 mL) butter

3 cups (750 mL) grated Havarti cheese

Chopped fresh chives or dill, for garnish (optional)

CASSEROLE DISH 101:
OTHERWISE KNOWN AS THE
BELOVED RETRO BAKING DISH

Casserole dishes can be used for everything from casseroles to crisps, and they're also great for serving dips to a larger crowd. They are available in a variety of shapes—typically round, oval, rectangular, and square—and capacities and can be used for baking, broiling, and roasting recipes. With sides typically less than 3 inches (8 cm) high, this shallow vessel allows foods to cook quickly and brown evenly.

WHAT TO LOOK FOR

GLASS CASSEROLE DISHES: These all-purpose dishes are made from a non-reactive material, making them ideal for egg casseroles and citrusy or tomato-based dishes. The non-porous surface doesn't absorb odours or flavours and is dishwasher-, oven-, and microwave-safe. Despite being oven-safe and made from tempered glass, it's not recommended that these dishes go under the broiler, as the abrupt temperature change can cause them to crack or shatter (thermal shock). They are available in a variety of sizes, and I like to keep 13- × 9-inch (33 × 23 cm), 11- × 7-inch (28 × 18 cm), and 8- or 9-inch (20 or 23 cm) square casserole dishes in my kitchen arsenal. Inexpensive, practical, and readily available, they can be purchased in many grocery, big box, department, discount, and housewares stores.

STONEWARE CASSEROLE DISHES: Stoneware is a non-reactive, all-purpose material that can be used to cook almost anything. Strong and durable, stoneware retains heat remarkably well and keeps food warm for serving. Look for dishes with side handles, which make them easy to lift and serve. These casserole dishes are almost always microwave-, oven-, freezer-, and dishwasher-safe, but you should check the manufacturer's instructions before using, especially if you want to broil a dish. All stoneware is not created equal, so you'll need to do some research if you have specific cooking requirements. Stoneware is often coated in a smooth, impermeable glaze that helps the bakeware resist stains and odours and also makes for easy cleaning. As I do with glass casserole dishes, I like to keep 13- × 9-inch (33 × 23 cm), 11- × 7-inch (28 × 18 cm), and 8- or 9-inch (20 or 23 cm) square dishes on hand and use them frequently. The price for stoneware casserole dishes varies quite dramatically, but you can assume that a highly regarded cookware brand will come with a price tag to match. Stoneware casserole dishes are readily available at most housewares and department stores and at high-end kitchen shops.

CARING FOR AND CLEANING CASSEROLE DISHES

The enamel surface of stoneware casserole dishes is scratch resistant and easy to clean. Cool the dish completely before cleaning, otherwise it's prone to cracking. Wash with hot, soapy water and dry thoroughly, or wash in the dishwasher on a full cleaning cycle. To remove baked-on, hard-to-remove residue, fill the casserole dish with warm, soapy water and soak for 30 minutes. Wash normally using a scrub brush as needed. As with Dutch ovens, do not use steel wool on these cooking vessels. For glass casserole dishes, scrubbing them quickly after each use makes for easier cleaning. The longer you leave them before cleaning, letting grease build up, the more difficult it is to remove. Pay attention to corners and handles, as they are more difficult to clean thoroughly and tend to become troublesome spots.

HOW TO STORE

Washed and dried casserole dishes can be stored nestled inside each other in a cupboard.

TOP TIPS FOR USE

- Do not use glass or stoneware casserole dishes on a stovetop or direct source of heat. Both are made from fragile materials and prone to shattering, cracking, and breaking, sometimes violently.
- Always preheat the oven before placing a glass casserole dish inside.
- Never put a cold stoneware casserole dish directly into a hot oven. Instead, place the dish in the oven as it preheats, allowing the dish and the oven to heat together, or let the dish come to room temperature on the counter before placing it in a hot oven.
- Before serving, use a thermometer to ensure that the centre of food is evenly heated (most casseroles should be heated to 165°F/75°C). Many casseroles use a combination of ingredients that cook at different rates, so you'll want to ensure that each is cooked properly before serving.
- If unsure of the volume of your casserole dish, check the capacity by filling the vessel with water, 1 cup (250 mL) at a time, until it reaches the top edge. If you need to substitute a casserole dish, look for one with equal volume to use as a replacement.

VEGETABLES, SIDES, AND SALADS

MY HOPE WITH this chapter is to encourage people to cook and be joyful about putting vegetables and simple side dishes on the table. And if they can be made in a single pot or pan, even better, don't you think? With a goal of making each of these side dishes just as flavourful as they are simple, while implementing less commonly used cooking techniques (such as roasting corn on the cob instead of boiling it, see page 179), feeding friends and family has never been easier. The dishes in this chapter are meant to both complete and complement your main meals, but they can also, in many cases, be their own main course. For example, the Kale Colcannon (page 175) and the Crispy Cauliflower with Raisins, Capers, and Lemony Bread Crumbs (page 171) are both perfect accompaniments to a simple roasted chicken but also are wonderful when served on their own, possibly topped with a pan-fried egg. The Twice-Baked Butternut Squash (page 192) is an ideal addition to a holiday meal but equally as delicious served as a vegetarian main dish.

QUINOA TABBOULEH WITH CHERRIES AND FETA

VEGETARIAN, MAKE AHEAD, KID FRIENDLY, QUICK COOKING, GLUTEN-FREE

Serves 4 to 6

2 cups (500 mL) water

1 cup (250 mL) quinoa

1½ teaspoons (7 mL) kosher salt, divided

¼ cup (60 mL) olive oil

¼ cup (60 mL) fresh lemon juice

4 green onions, thinly sliced

½ cup (125 mL) finely chopped fresh mint

½ cup (125 mL) finely chopped fresh parsley

1 English cucumber, diced

2 cups (500 mL) sweet cherries, pitted and halved

1 cup (250 mL) diced or crumbled feta cheese

In summer, I often struggle to come up with a seasonal salad because so many of the classics are made with tomatoes, which only makes sense seeing as they're in their prime at that time of year. The problem, for me, is that there is no food I dislike more than tomatoes. So, I'm always thinking up ways to replace tomatoes with other produce, and cherry tabbouleh was born. This salad certainly doesn't look like a traditional tabbouleh—with quinoa instead of bulgur and cherries in place of tomatoes—but really, the flavours are truly similar.

1. In a medium Dutch oven (4 to 6 quarts/3.8 to 5.7 L), bring the water to a boil. Rinse the quinoa well under cold, running water and add to the pot along with 1 teaspoon (5 mL) salt. Lower the heat and simmer, partially covered, for 15 minutes or until the grains are tender. Drain, if needed, and transfer to a bowl.

2. In a small jar, add the oil, lemon juice, and the remaining ½ teaspoon (2 mL) salt. Cover and shake to combine. Drizzle the dressing over the quinoa and stir well.

3. Add the green onions, mint, parsley, cucumber, and cherries to the bowl and mix well. Fold in the feta, check seasonings, and adjust if needed. Serve immediately or refrigerate for up to 2 days and serve cold.

CRISPY CAULIFLOWER WITH RAISINS, CAPERS, AND LEMONY BREAD CRUMBS

VEGETARIAN, KID FRIENDLY

Serves 4

Roasted cauliflower has become a favourite side dish in our house, and I consider this dish completely kid approved now that I've seen my kids lap it up like it was their final meal. The raisins, feta, and capers are completely optional, of course, but they do add a little something extra special to the dish. Feel free to simply roast the cauliflower as instructed and top it with the bread crumbs; that will work, too. In either case, this dish also makes for a quick vegetarian weeknight dinner when topped with a fried egg.

1. Preheat the oven to 425°F (220°C). Place the cauliflower on a rimmed sheet pan and drizzle with the oil. Add the thyme, salt, and red pepper flakes, then toss together with your hands to combine. Spread in an even layer and roast for 25 to 30 minutes or until the edges of the cauliflower florets are golden.
2. While the cauliflower is roasting, prepare the bread crumbs. Stir together the melted butter, panko, salt, pepper, and lemon zest. Set aside.
3. Remove the sheet pan from the oven and turn the oven to broil. Add the raisins, capers, and feta to the cauliflower and toss to combine. Sprinkle with the bread crumbs and broil for 2 to 4 minutes or until golden brown. Serve immediately or at room temperature.

For the cauliflower

1 medium head cauliflower (1½ to 2 pounds/675 to 900 g), cut into florets

3 tablespoons (45 mL) olive oil

4 sprigs thyme, leaves stripped

Kosher salt

¼ teaspoon (1 mL) crushed red pepper flakes

3 tablespoons (45 mL) golden raisins

1 tablespoon (15 mL) capers

3 tablespoons (45 mL) crumbled feta cheese

For the bread crumbs

3 tablespoons (45 mL) melted butter

¾ cup (175 mL) panko bread crumbs

½ teaspoon (2 mL) kosher salt

¼ teaspoon (1 mL) freshly ground black pepper

2 teaspoons (10 mL) lemon zest

HARVEST KALE PLATTER SALAD

Serves 6

VEGETARIAN, MAKE AHEAD, GLUTEN-FREE

½ cup + 2 tablespoons (155 mL) olive oil, divided

2 cups (500 mL) butternut squash, peeled and cut into ½-inch (1 cm) dice

4 medium shallots, peeled and quartered

Kosher salt

Freshly ground black pepper

1 bunch kale, rinsed and dried, ribs and stems removed, leaves thinly sliced crosswise

1 teaspoon (5 mL) Dijon mustard

2 tablespoons (30 mL) balsamic vinegar

1 tablespoon + 1 teaspoon (20 mL) pure maple syrup

1 apple, cored and thinly sliced

¼ cup (60 mL) dried cranberries

¼ cup (60 mL) pepitas

½ cup (125 mL) crumbled feta or goat cheese

Experience has taught me that people are immediately impressed when they see a large platter of salad come to the table instead of the expected salad bowl. Somehow it seems a little more special, when in fact serving salad on a platter can sometimes just be practical. It allows for heavier items, such as roasted squash and apples, to perch nicely on top of the greens instead of sinking into them. In this recipe, almost all of the components can—and should—be made in advance. If kale isn't your thing, this salad also works well with baby spinach. Just skip the bit about massaging the dressing into the greens and serve it on the side instead.

1. Preheat the oven to 425°F (220°C). Line a rimmed sheet pan with parchment paper.

2. On the prepared pan, toss together 2 tablespoons (30 mL) oil, squash, and shallots and arrange in a single layer. Season to taste with salt and pepper. Roast, turning occasionally, until the squash and shallots are tender and lightly golden, about 30 minutes. Remove the sheet pan from the oven and let cool completely.

3. Meanwhile, place the kale on a large platter. In a small bowl, whisk together the Dijon, vinegar, maple syrup, and the remaining ½ cup (125 mL) oil for the dressing; season with salt and pepper.

4. Drizzle ⅓ of the dressing over the kale. Using your fingers, "massage" the vinaigrette into the kale leaves, evenly coating them. Let rest for at least 15 minutes.

5. Scatter the apple, cranberries, pepitas, and feta over the kale and top with the roasted squash and shallots. Drizzle with 1 to 2 tablespoons (15 to 30 mL) more dressing and serve at once with extra dressing on the side.

KALE COLCANNON

VEGETARIAN, MAKE AHEAD, KID FRIENDLY,
QUICK COOKING, GLUTEN-FREE

Serves 4 to 6

There are as many colcannon recipes as there are cooks in Ireland, but this is the version I like best. The curly kale, green onions, and parsley bring a dose of colour and flavour to an otherwise ordinary potato dish, making this simple side equally at ease at a holiday dinner as it is at Wednesday night supper. I especially like it because it's an effortless way to get an extra serving of greens into my family members. Feel free to stir in 1 cup (250 mL) grated cheddar cheese for a cheesy version of the same dish.

4 medium russet or Yukon Gold
   potatoes, peeled and cut into 2-inch
   (5 cm) cubes
Kosher salt
5 tablespoons (75 mL) butter, divided
1 bunch curly kale, centre ribs removed
   and finely chopped
3 green onions, ends trimmed and
   thinly sliced
1 cup (250 mL) half-and-half (10%)
   cream
¼ cup (60 mL) chopped fresh parsley
Freshly ground black pepper

1. Place the potatoes in a medium Dutch oven (4 to 6 quarts/3.8 to 5.7 L) and cover by 1 inch (2.5 cm) with cold water. Add a large pinch of salt, bring to a boil, cover, and reduce heat to medium. Cook until the potatoes are fork tender, about 10 to 15 minutes.

2. Drain the potatoes and return the pot to the stove. Place 4 tablespoons (60 mL) butter in the pot to melt. Once the butter is melted, add the kale and cook until wilted, about 3 minutes. Add the green onions and cook for 1 minute more. Pour the cream into the pot and cook until warmed through.

3. Return the potatoes to the pot and mash with the back of a wooden spoon or potato masher. Add the parsley and season well with salt and pepper.

4. Spoon the warm potatoes into a serving bowl and top with the remaining 1 tablespoon (15 mL) butter. Serve hot.

Serves 4

2 tablespoons (30 mL) unsalted butter

½ cup (125 mL) orzo

1 small onion, finely chopped

¼ teaspoon (1 mL) turmeric

½ teaspoon (2 mL) garlic powder

½ cup (125 mL) basmati rice

1 bay leaf

2 cups (500 mL) Whole Chicken Broth (page 48) or low-sodium store-bought chicken broth

Kosher salt (optional)

2 tablespoons (30 mL) minced fresh parsley

RICE AND ORZO PILAF

This recipe is a great side dish for any meal, but it can also be eaten on its own. My family likes to warm up the leftovers and serve them for breakfast, topped with sunny-side-up eggs and plenty of hot sauce.

1. In a 10-inch (25 cm) cast iron, stainless steel, or non-stick skillet, melt the butter over medium heat. Add the orzo and onion and cook until the pasta is golden brown and the onion is soft and translucent, about 3 minutes. Sprinkle with the turmeric and garlic powder and stir; cook for 1 minute more.

2. Stir in the rice, bay leaf, and broth. Increase the heat to high and bring to a boil, then reduce the heat to medium-low. Quickly and carefully taste the liquid. If you feel it needs more salt, season to taste. Then partially cover the skillet and simmer until the rice is tender and the liquid has been absorbed, 20 to 25 minutes.

3. Remove the skillet from the heat and let stand for 5 minutes. Fluff with a fork, sprinkle with parsley, and serve hot.

ROASTED CORN ON THE COB WITH HERB BUTTER

Serves 6

I try to avoid creating a lot of steam in the kitchen during the summer months (my Stovetop Shrimp Boil on page 149 is definitely an exception), which is why I started roasting my corn on the cob. I know it probably sounds silly, but sometimes turning on the oven doesn't make the house as hot as cooking on the stovetop does, and when I'm feeding a crowd, this dish actually comes together quicker than if I had to bring an oversize pot of water to a boil. You can easily double or triple the recipe, if needed.

6 ears corn, husks and silks removed

½ cup (125 mL) unsalted butter, softened

3 tablespoons (45 mL) finely chopped fresh herbs (such as basil, dill, parsley, chives)

¾ teaspoon (4 mL) kosher salt

Pinch of cayenne pepper

2 green onions, white and light green parts only, thinly sliced

1. Preheat the oven to 400°F (200°C). Tear off 6 sheets of aluminum foil, each large enough to wrap 1 ear of corn.
2. In a small bowl, stir together the butter, herbs, salt, and cayenne. Using a butter knife or small spatula, spread the herb butter all over the corn, dividing it evenly between the 6 cobs. Tightly wrap the corn in the foil and place the cobs in a single layer on a rimmed sheet pan. Roast for 25 minutes.
3. Remove the sheet pan from the oven, open the foil packets, and sprinkle the corn with green onions. Serve at once.

TIP: You can double or triple the recipe for a large crowd, but you'll need to use more than 1 sheet pan to do so. Be sure not to stack the cobs on the pan, otherwise they won't cook completely.

Serves 6

6 tablespoons (90 mL) unsalted butter

2 pounds (900 g) Yukon Gold potatoes, peeled and sliced into 1-inch (2 cm) thick pieces

1 tablespoon (15 mL) fresh thyme leaves, plus extra for serving

Kosher salt

Freshly ground black pepper

¾ cup (175 mL) Whole Chicken Broth (page 48) or low-sodium store-bought chicken broth

3 garlic cloves, peeled and smashed

MELT-IN-YOUR-MOUTH POTATOES

In Britain, this crave-worthy potato dish is known as fondant potatoes, but here in North America, I daresay, they are barely known at all. In my opinion, thick-cut buttery potatoes slices that are crispy on the outside and creamy through the middle are definitely worthy of an introduction. These are truly my family's favourite potatoes and they pair just as well with a roast chicken for Sunday dinner as they do with a plate of scrambled eggs. Simply flavoured with thyme, garlic, salt, and pepper, this dish is a delicious upgrade from your typical roasties.

1. Position a rack in the top third of the oven and preheat to 500°F (260°C).

2. Place the butter in a 9- x 13-inch metal baking pan and melt in the oven while it preheats. Watch the butter carefully to ensure it doesn't burn. Remove the pan from the oven, add the potatoes and thyme leaves, and season with a generous pinch of salt and freshly ground pepper. Toss to combine.

3. Arrange the potatoes in a single layer over the bottom of the baking pan and bake for 15 minutes. Flip the potatoes and bake for 15 minutes more.

4. Remove the pan from the oven and pour the broth around the potatoes; scatter the garlic cloves over top. Bake for another 10 to 12 minutes or until the broth is almost completely absorbed.

5. To serve, transfer the potatoes to a platter and pour any liquid from the pan over top. Season with salt and pepper and sprinkle with extra thyme.

TIP: To make the dish vegetarian and vegan, replace the chicken broth with vegetable broth and the butter with olive oil.

CHEESY ORZO AND BROCCOLI

Serves 4

I keep orzo in my cupboard at all times. The petite pasta is quick cooking, which makes it a great alternative to spaghetti or penne when I'm in need of a speedy weeknight dinner or side dish. My older kids like to eat this with grilled sausages or chicken, but it also makes a mighty fine lunch for toddlers, especially if you're trying to avoid serving boxed macaroni and cheese to your family.

1 cup (250 mL) orzo

1½ cups (375 mL) finely chopped broccoli florets

¼ cup (60 mL) shredded Monterey Jack or cheddar cheese

2 tablespoons (30 mL) grated Parmesan cheese

1 tablespoon (15 mL) unsalted butter

Kosher salt

Freshly ground black pepper

1. Fill a medium Dutch oven (4 to 6 quarts/3.8 to 5.7 L) with salted water and bring to a boil. Add the orzo and cook for 7 minutes. Stir in the broccoli and cook for another 2 minutes or until the orzo is tender and the broccoli is soft. Reserve ½ cup (125 mL) of the cooking liquid, then drain really well; return the pasta and broccoli to the pot.

2. Add the Monterrey Jack, Parmesan, butter, and half of the reserved cooking liquid to the pot. Stir continuously until the "sauce" thickens, about 2 minutes. Add more reserved liquid as needed or until the sauce reaches the desired creaminess. Season to taste with salt and pepper and serve immediately.

ROASTED LENTIL AND WALNUT SALAD WITH GRAPES, SPINACH, AND GOAT CHEESE

Serves 2 to 4

1 can (19 ounces/540 mL) lentils, drained and rinsed (or 2 cups/500 mL cooked lentils)

½ cup (125 mL) walnut halves

¼ cup (60 mL) olive oil, divided

Kosher salt

Freshly ground black pepper

3 tablespoons (45 mL) red wine vinegar

1 teaspoon (5 mL) grainy Dijon mustard

1 teaspoon (5 mL) liquid honey

1 package (5 ounces/140 g) baby spinach (about 6 cups/1.5 L)

2 cups (500 mL) seedless red grapes, halved

½ cup (125 mL) crumbled goat cheese

Unless I have cooked lentils tucked away in my fridge, I always use the canned variety in this recipe in order to stick to the ease of one-pan cooking. Roasting the lentils makes them crisp just a little, and toasting the nuts at the same time adds more flavour to the salad. This is one of my favourite vegetarian dishes, and I'll confess that my husband and I don't have any problem polishing off the entire dish on our own when eating it as a main meal. If you aren't crazy about lentils, you can easily replace them with chickpeas here.

1. Preheat the oven to 425°F (220°C).
2. Place the lentils and walnuts in an enamel roasting pan and drizzle with 1 tablespoon (15 mL) oil. Season with salt and pepper and toss to combine. Bake for 10 minutes or until the lentils are slightly crisp and the walnuts are golden and fragrant. Remove the pan from the oven and let cool until slightly warmer than room temperature.
3. In the bottom of a salad or serving bowl, whisk together the remaining 3 tablespoons (45 mL) oil, red wine vinegar, mustard, and honey. Season to taste with salt and pepper.
4. Add the lentils, walnuts, spinach, and grapes to the bowl and toss to combine. Sprinkle the goat cheese over the salad and serve immediately.

SESAME STIR-FRIED VEGGIES

Serves 4

The great thing about a stir-fry is that it's one of the most flexible dishes you can make. You pretty much can toss in whatever vegetables you have available, so if you're missing something from the ingredients list below, don't fret; just use something else in its place. Because this is a quick-cooking dish and you're tossing things into the pan in rapid succession, it's critical that the ingredients are prepped and ready to go before you start cooking. Also, another secret to making good stir-fried veggies? Don't overcrowd the pan. If you do, the vegetables will sweat instead of fry.

½ cup (125 mL) tamari

2 tablespoons (30 mL) lime juice

3 tablespoons (45 mL) packed brown sugar

2 tablespoons (30 mL) cornstarch

2 teaspoons (10 mL) Sriracha hot sauce

2 tablespoons (30 mL) sesame oil

1 large yellow onion, cut into 1-inch (2.5 cm) chunks

1 head broccoli, cut into ¾-inch (2 cm) florets

1 red bell pepper, seeded and cut into 1-inch (2.5 cm) chunks

1 yellow bell pepper, seeded and cut into 1-inch (2.5 cm) chunks

1 zucchini, cut into 1-inch (2.5 cm) chunks

2 cloves garlic, grated or pressed

1 tablespoon (15 mL) grated peeled fresh ginger

1 tablespoon (15 mL) sesame seeds, for garnish

1. In a bowl, mix together the tamari, lime juice, brown sugar, cornstarch, and Sriracha. Set aside.
2. In a large cast iron, stainless steel, or non-stick skillet, heat the oil over medium-high heat. Add the onion and stir-fry, cooking until softened, about 1 to 2 minutes. Add the broccoli and cook for another 3 to 4 minutes or until crisp-tender. Next, add the peppers and zucchini and cook until all of the vegetables are tender, about another 3 to 4 minutes.
3. Add the garlic and ginger and cook for 30 seconds, stirring continuously. Pour the sauce over the vegetables and stir-fry for 1 minute more. Serve hot with a sprinkling of sesame seeds.

TIP: To make this side dish even faster to prepare, you can prep all the veggies and make the sauce up to 24 hours ahead of time. Keep in separate containers in the fridge.

SIMPLE SCALLOPED POTATOES WITH CELERIAC

VEGETARIAN, MAKE AHEAD, KID FRIENDLY, GLUTEN-FREE

Serves 6 to 8

2 tablespoons (30 mL) unsalted butter, divided

2 pounds (900 g) Yukon Gold potatoes, peeled and sliced into ¼-inch (0.5 cm) thick pieces

1½ pounds (675 g) celeriac, peeled and sliced into ¼-inch (0.5 cm) thick pieces

3 cloves garlic, grated or pressed

2 sprigs thyme, leaves stripped

Kosher salt

Freshly ground black pepper

2 cups (500 mL) heavy (35%) cream

½ cup (125 mL) grated Parmesan cheese

Also known as celery root, celeriac is a knobby root vegetable that's available in late fall through winter. Here it lends a slight celery flavour to the dish and adds a little lightness to balance the heavy potato. This warm and creamy dish is perfect for sharing with friends and family.

1. Preheat the oven to 375°F (190°C). Butter a 9- × 13-inch (23 × 33 cm) casserole dish with 1 tablespoon (15 mL) butter.

2. Layer ⅓ of the potato slices and ⅓ of the celeriac slices over the bottom of the prepared casserole dish. Sprinkle with ⅓ of the garlic and thyme, and season lightly with salt and pepper. Top with ⅓ of the cream. Repeat with the remaining ingredients, making 2 more layers and ending with the cream. Scatter the Parmesan over top and dot with the remaining 1 tablespoon (15 mL) butter. Cover the dish tightly with aluminum foil.

3. Bake for 1 hour. Carefully remove the foil and return the casserole dish to the oven, baking for another 25 to 30 minutes or until the potatoes are tender, the top is golden brown, and the sauce is bubbling. Remove the casserole dish from the oven and let stand for 10 minutes to set, then serve hot.

TIP: This dish can be made up to 1 day in advance. Cool completely, cover, and store in the refrigerator. To serve, let the dish come to room temperature and then reheat in a 300°F (150°C) oven until hot, about 20 minutes.

SKILLET STEAKHOUSE SALAD

MAKE AHEAD, KID FRIENDLY, QUICK COOKING,
GLUTEN-FREE

Serves 4

3 tablespoons (45 mL) olive oil, divided

¾ pound (340 g) fingerling potatoes, halved lengthwise

Kosher salt

Freshly ground black pepper

1 pound (450 g) strip or top sirloin steaks

½ cup (125 mL) sour cream

¼ cup (60 mL) buttermilk

1 cup (250 mL) crumbled blue cheese

2 tablespoons (30 mL) mayonnaise

1 teaspoon (5 mL) liquid honey

1 head green leaf or red leaf lettuce

1 cup (250 mL) cherry tomatoes, halved

1 English cucumber, diced

2 green onions, trimmed and thinly sliced

This is the salad you need to make for the meat and potato lover in your family. For me, that's pretty much everyone I live with, and while I enjoy those things too, I don't crave them in the same way my husband and sons do. I think this salad is a good representation of how we make everything in our life work: through compromise. There are good-for-you greens and veggies, plus pan-fried potatoes and steak, and it all comes together with a creamy, tangy blue cheese dressing. It's indulgent yet not, and pretty much pleases everyone at the table.

1. In a 10-inch (25 cm) cast iron, stainless steel, or non-stick skillet, heat 2 tablespoons (30 mL) oil over medium-high heat. Add the potatoes, cut side down, and cook until the bottoms are browned, about 5 minutes.

2. Turn the potatoes over and sprinkle with salt and pepper. Reduce the heat to medium and cook until potatoes are brown and tender, another 7 to 8 minutes. Remove the potatoes from the skillet and return the heat to medium-high.

3. Pat the steaks dry with paper towel and brush the remaining 1 tablespoon (15 mL) oil over both sides of the steaks. Generously season with salt and pepper. Add the steaks to the pan and cook until golden brown yet still pink inside (about 5 minutes per side for a medium steak). Transfer the steaks to a cutting board and let rest while preparing the salad.

4. While the steaks cook, make the dressing. In the carafe of a blender or in the bowl of a food processor fitted with a steel blade, combine the sour cream, buttermilk, blue cheese, mayonnaise, honey, ½ teaspoon (2 mL) salt, and ½ teaspoon (2 mL) pepper. Pulse until smooth.

5. To prepare the salad, divide the lettuce leaves evenly between 4 plates. Arrange the tomatoes and cucumber over top, and cover with potatoes. Thinly slice the steaks against the grain and divide between the plates, placing the meat down the middle of each salad. Garnish with green onions and serve with dressing on the side.

SWEET AND SAUCY BAKED BEANS

MAKE AHEAD, KID FRIENDLY

Serves 8

This is my sister's recipe; she makes this dish for most of her summer gatherings. I like that it uses canned beans and comes together in about an hour, unlike most baked bean recipes that require several hours of baking time. The leftovers reheat beautifully and could easily be used in the One-Pan English Breakfast (page 18).

1. Preheat the oven to 350°F (180°C).
2. In a large Dutch oven (7 to 9 quarts/6.6 to 8.5 L), cook the bacon over medium-high heat until crisp. Transfer to a plate lined with paper towel and drain all but 1 tablespoon (15 mL) of the fat from the pot. Add the onion, red pepper, and garlic and sauté until soft and translucent, about 3 minutes.
3. Add the beans to the pot and stir in the Worcestershire sauce, soy sauce, mustard, brown sugar, ketchup, and barbecue sauce. Simmer for 5 minutes. Return the bacon to the pot, cover, and bake in the oven for 45 minutes.
4. Remove the lid from the pot and bake, uncovered, for another 10 minutes. Remove the pot from the oven and let rest for 10 minutes before serving warm.

½ pound (225 g) bacon, chopped

1 medium onion, finely chopped

1 red pepper, finely chopped

2 cloves garlic, grated or pressed

2 cans (19 ounces/540 mL each) cannellini beans, drained and rinsed

2 cans (19 ounces/540 mL each) kidney beans, drained and rinsed

4 tablespoons (60 mL) Worcestershire sauce

2 tablespoons (30 mL) soy sauce

2 tablespoons (30 mL) yellow mustard

½ cup (125 mL) brown sugar

1 cup (250 mL) ketchup

1 cup (250 mL) barbecue sauce

Serves 4

2 small butternut squashes (about
    1½ pounds/675 g each)
2 tablespoons (30 mL) extra-virgin
    olive oil
Kosher salt
1 teaspoon (5 mL) fresh thyme leaves,
    plus extra for garnish
½ teaspoon (2 mL) freshly ground
    black pepper
¼ teaspoon (1 mL) ground nutmeg
6 cloves garlic, unpeeled
½ cup (125 mL) water
⅔ cup (170 mL) crumbled goat cheese
1 teaspoon (5 mL) liquid honey
¾ cup (175 mL) finely grated Parmesan
    cheese
3 tablespoons (45 mL) Italian-style
    breadcrumbs
1 tablespoon (15 mL) finely chopped
    sage leaves, plus extra for garnish

TIP: 1. To make the dish gluten-free,
eliminate the bread crumbs from the topping or use gluten-free bread crumbs in
place of the Italian-style variety. 2. To
make ahead, prep the recipe through
step 4. Cover and store in the refrigerator
for up to 2 days. To finish cooking, heat the
oven to 375°F (190°C) and bake for 25 to
30 minutes or until golden brown and
warm throughout. Serve as suggested.

TWICE-BAKED BUTTERNUT SQUASH

VEGETARIAN, MAKE AHEAD, KID FRIENDLY

These golden bell-shaped beauties are prepared in exactly the same way as their spud cousins, minus the rich and fatty additives that we've all come to love. When this dish is served alongside grilled meat, it's practically impossible to miss the heavy richness of the usual accompanying potato. To be perfectly honest, if I didn't spend my dinners accompanied by a band of boys, I would be happy to nosh on this dish paired with nothing more than a mixed green salad. Don't hesitate to serve this to vegetarians as a main course, and if you haven't already planned your fall and winter holiday meals, consider adding this to your menu for the squash-loving folks.

1. Preheat the oven to 425°F (220°C). Slice the squash in half lengthwise and scoop out and discard the seeds. In a 9- × 13-inch (23 × 33 cm) casserole dish, place the squash halves cut side up and score the flesh in a crosshatch pattern.

2. Drizzle the oil over the squash halves and sprinkle with a generous pinch of salt, fresh thyme leaves, pepper, and nutmeg. Scatter the garlic cloves over the squash and pour the water around the squash. Cover the casserole dish with aluminum foil and roast for 1 to 1½ hours or until the squash is tender when pierced with a fork. Lower the oven temperature to 375°F (190°C).

3. Squeeze the garlic cloves out of their skins into a large bowl. Using a soup spoon, scoop the squash flesh into the same bowl, leaving at least a ½-inch (1 cm) border around the squash shells so they will keep their shape. Add the goat cheese and honey to the bowl and mash everything together with a fork. Check seasonings and add more salt and pepper, if needed. If the squash lacks sweetness add a little more honey.

4. Remove the squash halves from the casserole dish and drain the dish of any remaining water. Return the halves back to the dish and spoon the squash mixture evenly among the 4 shells.

5. In a small bowl, stir together the Parmesan, breadcrumbs, and sage. Sprinkle over the squash halves.

6. Bake until golden brown and warm throughout, about 16 to 20 minutes. Garnish with sage leaves and fresh thyme and serve at once.

ENAMEL ROASTING PAN 101:
THE COOKWARE WE CAN'T
GET ENOUGH OF

Traditional roasting pans are designed for cooking large cuts of meat, such as a roast pork or a Thanksgiving turkey. They come in large rectangular or oval shapes with 2- to 4-inch (5 to 10 cm) high vertical sides, which help to keep the pan juices from overflowing in the oven. Sometimes they are outfitted with racks to keep the meat raised above the pan drippings as it cooks, but if your pan isn't equipped with one you can elevate the meat on a bed of vegetables or grains, or even a few thick-cut slices of bread. For the purposes of this book, I used an enamel roasting pan, which is typically smaller than its classic counterpart and often measures roughly 10 × 15 inches (25 × 38 cm) or smaller. This versatile pan can be used for roasting whole chickens, grains, and vegetables (Flat Roasted Chicken with Farro on page 123), baking sausages, making a hot water bath (Lemon Pudding Cake on page 213), and roasting tomato sauce (page 244). Timeless and fully functional, enamelware goes from stovetop to table seamlessly and travels well, making it perfect for carting to potlucks and picnics or for delivering food to a friend in need of a homemade meal. The curled rim and rounded corners make it an easy pan to carry.

WHAT TO LOOK FOR

Choose a roasting pan based on how you plan to use it. If cooking Thanksgiving dinner for twenty-three people is on your fall agenda, be sure to purchase an oversize roasting pan that can accommodate a bird big enough to feed your crowd. If everyday weeknight dinners for four are more your speed, a basic enamel roasting pan is a great option. Oven-safe up to 500°F (260°C), most of these pans can also be used on an electric or gas stovetop. As always, be sure to check the manufacturer's instructions before cooking with a roasting pan. Enamel roasting pans are also freezer- and dishwasher-safe, but porcelain enamel cookware should never be used in a microwave. These pans are not as readily available as some of the other cookware used in this book. I tend to purchase my new pans online, but have spotted them in some independent boutique stores that have gourmet kitchen sections. The price varies, but new pieces are more of an investment than those you can score at an antique market,

where enamelware is often readily available. One note of caution: experience has taught me that if you are purchasing a new enamel roasting pan, reliable brands like Falcon are worth the extra money. All enamelware are not created equal, and I have definitely picked up my fair share of duds.

CARING FOR AND CLEANING ENAMEL
ROASTING PANS

Being glass-coated steel, enamelware can chip easily if dropped or banged around too aggressively. However, according to Falcon, the premier producer of enamelware, the exposed steel oxidizes, rendering the cookware safe to use. Besides, the beaten-up look just adds to its charm, and despite the dents and divets it may develop, the pans remain useful and are full of character. If chips are large and on the bottom of the pan, you may want to avoid using it, as it's possible that small pieces of enamel will end up in your food. To prevent any chips along the rim from rusting, regularly rub in a small amount of cooking oil (not olive oil), as you would with a cast iron skillet. White enamelware is known to stain, but lemon juice or baking soda can often remove it. Brush a quarter-size amount of either onto the pan and the stains should magically disappear. Soak your pans in warm, soapy water to help remove baked-on food, but avoid using abrasive sponges and cleaners, as they can scratch the coating. Instead, scrub with a soft-bristled cleaning brush or dishcloth. Metal utensils are safe for this type of pan, but rubber, wood, and heat-resistant plastic are best.

HOW TO STORE

Enamelware roasting pans are designed to fit flush inside one another, making them smartly stackable. A benefit of this design is that they take up a limited amount of space in a cupboard or on a shelf. If you're worried about the pans rubbing against one another and scratching the surface, you can slip a piece of paper towel between the pans to protect them.

TOP TIPS FOR USE

- Enamelware is freezer friendly and perfect for batch cooking.
- Do not use enamelware in the microwave.
- Although enamelware may seem tough as nails (and it kind of is), it's also not completely immune to chips, so be gentle with your pans.
- To protect against scratching, avoid using steel wool when cleaning.

SWEET STUFF

IF YOU GAZE down the baking aisle of any major supermarket, it's easy to see the shelves bulging with "just add water" mixes ready to be baked. With so many selections available, it's clear that consumers are looking for a simplified way to put something sweet and semi-homemade on the table. Fortunately, one-pan baked goods offer the same unfussy, low-stress options as those packaged sweets in the grocery store. With a few humble baking pans, you will be well on your way to making snacks for the kids, such as Baked Apple Spice Doughnuts (page 198), or cakes for all of your special occasions, including my Single Layer Chocolate Celebration Cake (page 220). My Sour Cream Apple Slab Pie (page 215) requires one small sheet pan instead of two or three pie plates, making it easy to serve dessert to a large crowd. Baking in a skillet makes quick work of the Salted Chocolate Tahini Skillet Blondies (page 210), allowing you to forego the scooping and spooning of the dough by simply pressing it into a pan. The foolproof options are limitless!

Makes 12 doughnuts

For the doughnuts

6 tablespoons (90 mL) canola oil, plus extra for pan

1 cup (250 mL) all-purpose flour

½ cup (125 mL) whole wheat flour

¾ teaspoon (4 mL) baking powder

¾ teaspoon (4 mL) ground cinnamon

½ teaspoon (2 mL) fine sea salt

¼ teaspoon (1 mL) baking soda

¼ teaspoon (1 mL) grated nutmeg

¼ teaspoon (1 mL) ground cardamom

2 large eggs, room temperature, lightly beaten

¾ cup (175 mL) packed brown sugar

½ cup (125 mL) pressed sweet apple cider or apple juice

⅓ cup (85 mL) unsweetened applesauce

1 teaspoon (5 mL) vanilla bean paste or pure vanilla extract

For the topping

½ cup (125 mL) cane sugar

1½ teaspoon (7 mL) cinnamon

3 tablespoons (45 mL) unsalted butter, melted

BAKED APPLE SPICE DOUGHNUTS

VEGETARIAN, MAKE AHEAD, KID FRIENDLY, QUICK COOKING

When it comes to hosting Thanksgiving, something we've been doing since 2001, not one person around our table forgets that the kids always partake in a eating-doughnuts-on-a-string competition. To this day, my very grown-up teenagers still look forward to devouring those doughnuts *sans* hands, and my toddler is just old enough to join in, so you can be sure we'll be repeating this activity for many, many years to come. These baked doughnuts keep the sugar highs from soaring amid the excitement of the holiday and are great for older kids to bake on their own.

1. Preheat the oven to 400°F (200°C). Generously oil a 6-well doughnut pan and set aside (you'll be making the doughnuts in 2 batches, wiping the pan clean and brushing it with more oil before filling with the remaining batter).

2. In a large bowl, stir together the all-purpose and whole wheat flours, baking powder, cinnamon, salt, baking soda, nutmeg, and cardamom. Create a well in the centre of the bowl and add the oil, eggs, brown sugar, apple cider, applesauce, and vanilla. Stir until just combined.

3. Transfer the batter to a large zip top bag. Seal and snip the end off one of the bottom corners to create a piping bag. You'll want this hole to be similar in size to a large round piping tip, as the batter is thick.

4. Pipe the batter into the prepared doughnut pan, filling the wells to within ¼ inch (0.5 cm) of the rim. Bake for 10 minutes, remove the pan from the oven, and let sit for 3 to 5 minutes before turning the doughnuts out onto a cooling rack. Wipe the pan clean, brush with oil, and repeat with the remaining batter.

5. Meanwhile, mix the sugar and cinnamon. Brush the doughnuts liberally with the melted butter, sprinkle all over with the cinnamon sugar, and return to the cooling rack. Doughnuts are best served slightly warm on the day they are made, but will keep, covered, at room temperature, for 2 days.

TIP: If you have 2 doughnut pans, you can certainly bake all of the doughnuts at the same time.

CARROT CAKE SNACKING LOAF WITH CREAM CHEESE FROSTING

Serves 8 to 10

I am smitten with single layer snacking cakes. Popularized by Betty Crocker in the 1970s, their claim to fame was that they were so moist they couldn't crumble. Fast and foolproof, they were ideal for whipping up between taking the kids to the dentist and handing in an assignment to one's editor. My version of carrot cake boasts these qualities, with a slightly more wholesome list of ingredients. It's perfect for pairing with a cup of tea or coffee, packing into a school lunchbox, or serving when you have an unexpected visit from an old friend. As with many baking recipes, the eggs should be at room temperature, but in the spirit of keeping this recipe simple, I'm not going to suggest you pull them from the fridge a few hours before you bake. Instead, soak the cold eggs in warm water for a minute or two to speed them along.

1. Preheat the oven to 350°F (180°C). Grease an 8½- × 4½-inch (21 × 11 cm) loaf pan and line with parchment paper, leaving a 2-inch (5 cm) overhang on the 2 long sides.

2. In a medium bowl, stir together the oil, yogurt, eggs, vanilla, and orange zest until well mixed. In a second bowl, whisk the flour, brown sugar, baking soda, cinnamon, baking powder, salt, and nutmeg. Add the dry ingredients, carrots, and pineapple to the bowl with the wet ingredients and gently mix to combine. Do not overmix the batter. Fold in the raisins and walnuts, if using.

3. Scrape the batter into the prepared pan. Tap the pan on the counter a few times to remove any air bubbles. Bake for 40 to 50 minutes or until the top of the cake is firm and golden brown. Remove the pan from the oven and let cool for 10 minutes. Using the paper overhang, loosen the sides of the cake and remove it from the pan. Allow to cool completely on a wire rack before icing.

4. To make the frosting, in a medium bowl, combine the cream cheese and butter and blend with an electric mixer until smooth. Add the powdered sugar and mix at low speed until combined. Stir in the vanilla and mix again. Spread the frosting on the cooled cake before slicing.

For the snacking loaf

⅓ cup (85 mL) canola oil

⅓ cup (85 mL) plain yogurt

2 large eggs

2 teaspoons (10 mL) vanilla bean paste or pure vanilla extract

1 teaspoon (5 mL) grated orange zest

1 cup (250 mL) all-purpose flour

¾ cup (175 mL) packed brown sugar

1 teaspoon (5 mL) baking soda

1 teaspoon (5 mL) ground cinnamon

½ teaspoon (2 mL) baking powder

½ teaspoon (2 mL) kosher salt

¼ teaspoon (1 mL) freshly ground nutmeg

1½ cups (375 mL) grated carrots

½ cup (125 mL) crushed pineapple, drained

½ cup (125 mL) golden raisins (optional)

½ cup (125 mL) chopped walnuts (optional)

For the frosting

½ cup (125 mL) cream cheese, room temperature (4 ounces/110 g)

¼ cup (60 mL) unsalted butter, room temperature

1 cup (250 mL) powdered sugar

½ teaspoon (2 mL) vanilla bean paste or pure vanilla extract

Makes 2 dozen cookies

1 cup (250 mL) whole wheat flour

½ cup (125 mL) all-purpose flour

1 teaspoon (5 mL) ground ginger

1 teaspoon (5 mL) cinnamon

½ teaspoon (2 mL) nutmeg

1 tablespoon (15 mL) cocoa powder

½ teaspoon (2 mL) kosher salt

1 teaspoon (5 mL) baking soda

½ cup (125 mL) unsalted butter, room temperature

½ cup (125 mL) packed demerara or dark brown sugar

½ cup (125 mL) molasses

⅓ cup (85 mL) evaporated cane or granulated sugar, for rolling

SPICED COCOA MOLASSES COOKIES

VEGETARIAN, MAKE AHEAD, KID FRIENDLY, WHOLE GRAIN

In recent years, I've implemented a cozy and calm approach to the holiday season. Instead of having a hyper-organized plan in place for what to make and when to make it, I keep things tasty by reducing my must-make list to nothing but the very essential, one of which is cookies. These cookies are one of our favourite recipes, and they bring the best flavours of the season—chocolate, ginger, cinnamon, and molasses—to the table in a relatively wholesome way. I've been making these for years, tweaking them a little each time, and I think this version is the best. Don't relegate these to the winter holidays, though; they're also perfect for packing into school lunches.

1. Combine the whole wheat and all-purpose flours, ginger, cinnamon, nutmeg, cocoa powder, salt, and baking soda in a medium mixing bowl; set aside.

2. In the bowl of an electric mixer, cream the butter and brown sugar on medium speed until fluffy, 4 to 5 minutes. Scrape down the bowl, add the molasses, and mix until combined.

3. Add the flour mixture to the butter mixture and mix until just combined. Cover the bowl with plastic wrap and refrigerate for at least 1 hour or overnight.

4. Preheat the oven to 325°F (160°C) and line a rimmed sheet pan with parchment paper. Place the cane sugar in a small bowl. Shape the dough into 1-inch (2.5 cm) balls and roll them around in the sugar. Place half of the balls on the prepared pan, spacing them 2 inches (5 cm) apart; return the remaining cookie dough balls to the refrigerator to keep cool. Bake for 10 to 12 minutes or until the tops of the cookies begin to crack and the edges are set.

5. Remove the sheet pan from the oven and let cool for 15 minutes. The cookies will harden as they cool. Transfer to a wire rack and repeat with the remaining balls of dough. Store in a covered container at room temperature for up to 3 days or in the freezer for 3 months.

VARIATION: Using a rubber spatula, stir ½ cup (125 mL) chopped chocolate into the batter in step 3 after the flour mixture has been added.

MAPLE WALNUT BISCOTTI

Makes about 3 dozen biscotti

In addition to traditional shortbread, jam thumbprint cookies, and my family's favourite peanut butter balls, I recently added biscotti to my list of holiday must-make cookies. This twice-baked creation is simple to prepare and freezes beautifully, meaning you can make a few batches ahead of time and tuck them away until needed. Biscotti also happens to travel well, making it a wonderful edible gift for hostesses or family members that live far away.

2 cups (500 mL) walnuts

2 large eggs

½ cup (125 mL) granulated sugar

½ cup (125 mL) firmly packed brown sugar

¼ cup (60 mL) pure maple syrup

¼ to ½ teaspoon (1 to 2 mL) maple flavour (optional)

⅓ cup (85 mL) butter, melted

2½ cups (625 mL) all-purpose flour

2 teaspoons (10 mL) baking powder

½ teaspoon (2 mL) salt

2 tablespoons (30 mL) coarse sugar

1. Preheat the oven to 350°F (180°C) and line a rimmed sheet pan with parchment paper.
2. Toast the walnuts by spreading them in a single layer on the prepared pan and baking for 8 to 10 minutes or until they're lightly golden brown and fragrant. Remove the pan from the oven and let cool for 1 minute, then roughly chop the nuts. Set aside both the walnuts and the sheet pan.
3. In a medium bowl, using a handheld or stand mixer, beat together the eggs, granulated and brown sugars, maple syrup, and maple flavour (if using) until well combined, 2 to 3 minutes. Add the melted butter and beat until smooth.
4. Sift the flour, baking powder, and salt over the wet ingredients and mix with a rubber spatula. Stir in the nuts.
5. Divide the dough in half and, and using dampened fingers, shape each portion into a 10- × 3-inch (25 × 8 cm) rectangle, approximately 1 inch (2.5 cm) thick. Smooth the top and sides, adding more water to your fingers if needed, to prevent them from sticking. Place the dough on the reserved sheet pan and sprinkle the tops with coarse sugar.
6. Bake the biscotti dough for 30 minutes. Remove the pan from the oven and let cool for 10 minutes. Using a sharp chef's knife or serrated bread knife, cut the dough on the bias (at a 45-degree angle to the length of the cookie) into ½-inch (1 cm) thick slices.
7. Place the slices close together and balanced upright (rather than laying them flat) on the sheet pan. Bake for another 10 to 15 minutes or until the sides of the cookies are beginning to brown. Remove the pan from the oven and let cool completely. Cookies can be stored at room temperature in an airtight container for up to 1 week.

FUDGY RASPBERRY SWIRL BROWNIES

VEGETARIAN, MAKE AHEAD, KID FRIENDLY

Makes 12 brownies

½ cup (125 mL) butter

1½ cups (375 mL) semi-sweet
  chocolate chips, divided

3 large eggs

1 cup (250 mL) granulated sugar

1 teaspoon (5 mL) vanilla bean paste or
  pure vanilla extract

⅔ cups (170 mL) all-purpose flour

Pinch of salt

½ cup (125 mL) raspberry jam

My friend Tess is a mentor to me in many ways. She's a few years ahead of me in both her career and her parenting journey, and I've sought out her advice and wisdom more times that I can count. When I mentioned in passing that I wanted to include another chocolate-based recipe in *Oven to Table*, she immediately texted me a photo of a handwritten recipe in scrolling cursive titled "My Raspberry Swirl Brownies." I promptly baked them and think you should, too. A dessert (and a friend) doesn't get any easier, or sweeter, than this.

1. Preheat the oven to 350°F (180°C). Lightly grease an 8-inch (20 cm) square baking pan and line with parchment paper, leaving a 2-inch (5 cm) overhang on 2 sides of the pan.

2. In a medium microwave-safe mixing bowl, melt the butter and 1 cup (250 mL) chocolate chips as follows. Heat in the microwave on medium-high for 1 minute. Remove the bowl from the microwave and stir. Repeat heating at 15- to 20-second intervals, stirring in between, until the mixture is completely melted and smooth.

3. Whisk in the eggs, sugar, and vanilla until well blended. Using a rubber spatula, stir in the flour and salt. Carefully fold in the remaining ½ cup (125 mL) chocolate chips and pour into the prepared pan, spreading the mixture evenly into the corners.

4. Drop spoonfuls of jam over the brownie batter. Using a knife, swirl the jam through the batter. Bake for 35 to 40 minutes or until the top is set. Remove the pan from the oven and let cool completely on a wire rack. Using the parchment overhang, lift the brownies from the pan and cut into squares.

PRETZEL MAGIC BARS

VEGETARIAN, MAKE AHEAD, KID FRIENDLY, QUICK COOKING

Makes 20 bars

Like those retro seven-layer magic bars we all love and devour, this version is made with a few of my favourite bar snacks, such as pretzel sticks and crunchy almonds, instead of chopped pecans and crushed graham crackers. I daresay I like these better, with their thick base and salty-sweet flavour, and can confirm that they are just as easy to make as the version our mothers baked up in the 1970s. These are the perfect make-ahead dessert for your next party!

¾ cup (175 mL) unsalted butter, melted, plus more for pan

5½ cups (1.25 L) pretzel sticks, divided

¼ cup (60 mL) granulated sugar

1 can (10 ounces/300 mL) sweetened condensed milk

1½ cups (375 mL) almonds, chopped

1 cup (250 mL) semi-sweet chocolate chips

½ cup (125 mL) shredded sweetened coconut

1. Preheat the oven to 350°F (180°C). Butter a 9-inch (23 cm) square baking pan and line with parchment paper, leaving a 2-inch (5 cm) overhang on all sides. Butter the parchment paper.

2. Place 4½ cups (1.13 L) pretzels in the bowl of a food processor fitted with a steel blade and pulse until the texture resembles crushed graham crackers. Transfer to a bowl and stir in the sugar and melted butter until well combined. Transfer to the pan, spreading evenly, and pack down flat with the bottom of a measuring cup.

3. Drizzle the condensed milk evenly over the crust. Sprinkle evenly with almonds, chocolate chips, and coconut. Using your hands, lightly crush the remaining 1 cup (250 mL) pretzels and scatter them over top, gently pressing them into the condensed milk.

4. Bake until the chocolate melts and the condensed milk bubbles and becomes golden, 20 to 22 minutes. Remove the pan from the oven, place it on a wire rack, and let cool completely. Then refrigerate until the chocolate is set, about 30 minutes.

5. Run a small paring knife or spatula around the sides of the pan and, using the parchment overhang, transfer the bars to a cutting board. Cut into 20 squares.

Serves 6 to 8

1½ cups (375 mL) all-purpose flour

1 teaspoon (5 mL) baking powder

½ teaspoon (2 mL) kosher salt

½ cup (125 mL) unsalted butter

1½ cups (375 mL) packed brown sugar

1 cup (250 mL) well-stirred tahini

2 large eggs

2 teaspoons (10 mL) vanilla bean paste
or pure vanilla extract

1 cup (250 mL) chopped dark chocolate chunks or chocolate chips
(about 6 ounces/170 g)

½ teaspoon (2 mL) flaky sea salt

Vanilla ice cream, for serving (optional)

SALTED CHOCOLATE TAHINI
SKILLET BLONDIES

VEGETARIAN, MAKE AHEAD, KID FRIENDLY

I'm a fan of both dense, fudgy brownies and chewy chocolate chip cookies, and a blondie is what you'd get if the two united. This variation is spiked with tahini, adding an underlying nutty richness from the sesame paste, and embellished with chopped chocolate and finished with flaky sea salt—and the combination is both sweet and salty. In other words, it's totally amazing. Tahini is a Middle Eastern ingredient that is now available in most grocery stores. Look for it where you would find vinegars and condiments, or in the international aisle if there is one.

1. Preheat the oven to 350°F (180°C).

2. In a medium bowl, whisk together the flour, baking powder, and kosher salt; set aside.

3. In a 10-inch (25 cm) cast iron skillet, melt the butter over medium-low heat. Once the butter has completely melted, add the brown sugar and whisk together until it dissolves, about 1 minute.

4. Pour the butter mixture into the flour mixture. Add the tahini, eggs, and vanilla. Carefully mix with a wooden spoon or rubber spatula until just combined. Allow to cool slightly.

5. Fold the chopped chocolate into the dough. Transfer the dough back to the buttery skillet and press it evenly into the pan. Sprinkle with the sea salt, and bake for 25 to 30 minutes or until the blondie is golden brown on top and the centre is set. You'll know it's done when a cake tester or toothpick inserted into the middle of the blondie comes out clean.

6. Remove the skillet from the oven and let cool for at least 30 to 45 minutes before slicing. Slice into wedges like a pie, or cut into as many squares as desired. Top each serving with vanilla ice cream, if using. Blondies will keep for 3 days in an airtight container at room temperature.

LEMON PUDDING CAKE

Serves 4 to 6

It seems strange that lemon is so strongly associated with spring when citrus fruits burst onto the scene in winter, just when the last of the fall fruits have been tucked away for the season and we're all weary of seeing apples, cranberries, and pears on our plates. Lemons bring some much needed brightness to our long, grey days and zhoosh up dessert in a simple yet exciting way. This recipe is the marriage of two great desserts: pudding and cake. The cake portion rises to the top of the casserole dish, making room for a creamy pudding-like sauce to form on the bottom. It can be served completely unadorned, but I like to throw blackberries into mine every once in a while. For serving, sprinkle the top with a blanket of powdered sugar snow.

¼ cup (60 mL) unsalted butter, softened

1 cup (250 mL) sugar, divided

3 large eggs, separated

Grated zest of 1 lemon

⅓ cup (85 mL) all-purpose flour

¼ teaspoon (1 mL) salt

1 cup (250 mL) milk

¼ cup (60 mL) fresh lemon juice

1½ cups (375 mL) fresh blackberries (optional)

Powdered sugar, for serving (optional)

1. Preheat the oven to 350°F (180°C). Lightly grease an 8- × 8-inch (20 × 20 cm) or similar-size casserole dish. Fill a tea kettle with water and bring to a boil.

2. In a bowl, cream the butter and ¾ cup (175 mL) sugar until combined but grainy and light in colour. Whisk in the egg yolks and lemon zest. The butter mixture will loosen and look more like a batter. Stir in the flour and salt. Add the milk and lemon juice and mix until just combined.

3. In a second bowl, beat the egg whites until soft peaks form. Gradually add the remaining ¼ cup (60 mL) sugar, 1 tablespoon (15 mL) at a time, beating constantly until stiff peaks form.

4. Gently fold the egg whites into the lemon mixture. To do this, heap a large spoonful of egg whites into the lemon mixture and stir to combine. This will lighten the batter, making it easier to fold in the remaining egg whites. Then, using a rubber spatula, gently fold in the remaining egg whites. Continue working carefully until the mixture is blended, taking care not to overmix the batter. Next, fold in the blackberries (if using), and pour the batter into the prepared dish. Place the casserole dish into a 9- × 13-inch (23 × 33 cm) or similar-size roasting pan.

5. Place the roasting pan on the oven rack and pour in hot water from the kettle until the level reaches halfway up the sides of the casserole dish. Bake 30 to 35 minutes or until the top is lightly browned. Remove the casserole dish from the water and let cool for 10 minutes. Sprinkle the cake with powdered sugar, if using.

SOUR CREAM APPLE SLAB PIE

VEGETARIAN, MAKE AHEAD, KID FRIENDLY

Serves 20

This pie might be the greatest. The crust is flaky and the filling, while not traditional, is sweet and creamy, the perfect complement to the tender apple pieces. If that isn't enough to convince you of this pie's merits, the brown sugar topping just might. It's also simple and speedy, and the intoxicating scent permeates the house in a way no scented candle can. I've rarely served this pie without accolades; it's just that good. This pie really benefits from plenty of chilling time (at least two hours), so take that into consideration when planning to make this recipe.

1. To make the topping, in a bowl, stir together the butter, sugar, cinnamon, flour, and salt until the mixture is well combined and crumbly. Cover and chill in the refrigerator until needed. This step can be done a few hours or a day in advance.

2. To make the pie dough, in a large bowl, stir together the flour and salt. Cut in the butter with a pastry blender or your fingers until the mixture resembles coarse rolled oats. In a glass measuring cup, add the egg yolk and lemon juice and then fill to the ½-cup (125 mL) mark with cold water. Whisk to combine. Add the liquid to the large bowl, a bit at a time, blending it lightly with a fork. Finish by mixing the dough gently with your hands. Shape the dough into a disc and wrap tightly in plastic wrap. Refrigerate for several hours or overnight.

3. When you are ready to bake the pie, roll out the dough on a lightly floured work surface (or between 2 large, floured pieces of parchment paper) to ¼-inch (0.5 cm) thickness. Fit the dough into a 10- × 15-inch (25 × 38 cm) rimmed sheet pan, pressing it evenly into the bottom and corners of the pan. Trim the excess pastry, leaving a ½-inch (1 cm) overhang, and fold the overhang under itself, pressing it onto the rim of the sheet pan. Use your fingers to create a scalloped edge, if desired. Chill in the refrigerator until firm, at least 1 hour.

4. To make the filling, in a large bowl, whisk together the sour cream, eggs, sugar, flour, vanilla, and salt until the mixture is completely smooth. Add the apple slices and stir.

5. Spoon the filling into the chilled pie shell and crumble the topping evenly over it. Chill for at least 1 hour and up to 8 hours, if desired.

Recipe continues . . .

For the crumble topping

5 tablespoons (75 mL) unsalted butter, softened
½ cup (125 mL) brown sugar
1½ teaspoons (7 mL) ground cinnamon
3 tablespoons (45 mL) all-purpose flour
Pinch of kosher salt

For the pie dough

3 cups (750 mL) all-purpose flour
¾ teaspoon (4 mL) kosher salt
1 cup (250 mL) cold unsalted butter
1 large egg yolk
1 teaspoon (5 mL) fresh lemon juice
Cold water

For the filling

2 cups (500 mL) sour cream
3 large eggs
1⅓ cup (335 mL) granulated sugar
5 tablespoons (75 mL) all-purpose flour
2 teaspoons (10 mL) vanilla bean paste or pure vanilla extract
½ teaspoon (2 mL) salt
6 or 7 large Granny Smith apples, peeled, cored, and thinly sliced
Optional toppings for serving: whipped cream, vanilla ice cream

6. When you are ready to bake the pie, heat the oven to 350°F (180°C). Place a piece of aluminum foil on the bottom rack of the oven. Slide the sheet pan onto the middle rack of the oven. Bake for 75 to 90 minutes or until the crust is golden brown and the filling is bubbling. You may need to put a piece of aluminum foil over the pie during the last 15 minutes of baking time to prevent the top from burning.

7. Remove the sheet pan from the oven, transfer to a wire rack, and let cool completely. Slice the pie and serve warm or at room temperature topped with whipped cream or vanilla ice cream, if using.

TIP: Double the pie dough if you want to make a lid or lattice top for the pie. Alternatively, you can create cut-outs (hearts, stars, or circles) with the dough to decorate the top of the pie.

RUSTIC STONE FRUIT CROSTATA WITH CORNMEAL CRUST

Serves 6 to 8

This rustic summer dessert is nothing more than a piece of rolled-out dough piled high with peak-season produce. This dessert practically insists that you check your perfectionist tendencies at the door, allowing you to have a little fun with this free-form pastry. Baked on a standard sheet pan, no two crostatas ever look the same, and it's that unpolished look that make this sweet so approachable. While I like to brush some jam over the inside of my pastry before piling on the fruit, that move isn't essential. I think it boosts the overall flavour of the recipe, but it will be just as tasty without.

1. In the bowl of a food processor fitted with a steel blade, pulse together the flour, cornmeal, sugar, and salt. Sprinkle the cold, cubed butter over top and pulse 4 or 5 times or until the mixture resembles dried oats.
2. Add the water, 1 tablespoon (15 mL) at a time, pulsing until the dough begins to hold together. If you need more than 4 tablespoons (60 mL) water, sprinkle in the additional water in tiny amounts so the dough doesn't get too wet.
3. Gather the dough into a ball, flatten into a disc, and wrap in plastic wrap. Chill in the refrigerator for 30 minutes or up to 1 day.
4. Remove the chilled dough from the refrigerator and let sit at room temperature for 15 minutes. Lightly flour a piece of parchment paper and roll out the dough to a 12- to 14-inch (30 to 35 cm) circle, turning the dough often to prevent it from sticking. Slide a rimmed sheet pan under the piece of parchment paper and return the dough to the refrigerator. Chill the dough on the pan until you are ready to assemble the crostata.
5. Preheat the oven to 400°F (200°C). Place the sliced stone fruit in a medium mixing bowl and stir in the orange zest, cornstarch, vanilla, and 3 tablespoons (45 mL) sugar. Taste the fruit; if it isn't sweet enough or to your liking, add more sugar, 1 tablespoon (15 mL) at a time, until it reaches the desired sweetness.
6. Remove the dough from the refrigerator. Spread the jam over the pastry, covering it evenly to the edges. Pile the fruit in the centre of the dough, leaving a 2-inch (5 cm) border around the sides of the pastry. The fruit should be slightly domed in the middle.

Recipe continues . . .

For the crust

1¾ cups (425 mL) all-purpose flour

¼ cup (60 mL) medium grind cornmeal

2 tablespoons (30 mL) cane or granulated sugar

¾ teaspoon (4 mL) salt

¾ cup + 2 tablespoons (205 mL) chilled unsalted butter, cut into ½-inch (1 cm) cubes

4 to 6 tablespoons (60 to 90 mL) ice cold water

For the filling

6 cups (1.5 L) stone fruit (such as plums, peaches, nectarines), pitted and sliced ½ inch (1 cm) thick

1 teaspoon (5 mL) grated orange zest (from 1 medium orange)

1½ teaspoons (7 mL) cornstarch

1 teaspoon (5 mL) vanilla bean paste or pure vanilla extract

3 to 6 tablespoons (45 to 90 mL) granulated sugar

½ cup (125 mL) apricot jam

1 large egg, lightly beaten

1 tablespoon (15 mL) coarse sugar

Whipped cream, for serving (optional)

7. Using the piece of parchment to assist, fold up the edge of the dough around the fruit. Make a fold every 2 inches (5 cm) or so, creating a creased rim of dough around the edges of the fruit. Using a pastry brush, lightly brush the egg over the crust and then sprinkle it with the coarse sugar.

8. Bake for 45 to 55 minutes or until the crust is golden brown and the fruit is bubbling. Remove the sheet pan from the oven and let cool for at least 15 to 20 minutes before serving. Serve with whipped cream, if using.

SINGLE LAYER CHOCOLATE CELEBRATION CAKE

Serves 12 to 20

For the cake

1½ cups (375 mL) all-purpose flour

½ cup (125 mL) cocoa powder

1½ cups (375 mL) brown sugar

1 teaspoon (5 mL) baking powder

1 teaspoon (5 mL) baking soda

½ teaspoon (2 mL) kosher salt

4 tablespoons (60 mL) butter, melted

4 tablespoons (60 mL) canola oil

2 large eggs, lightly beaten

1 cup (250 mL) black coffee, room temperature

1 cup (250 mL) buttermilk

1 teaspoon (5 mL) vanilla bean paste or pure vanilla extract

For the frosting

2 cups (500 mL) milk chocolate chips

1 cup (250 mL) sour cream

1 teaspoon (5 mL) vanilla bean paste or pure vanilla extract

Optional topping for decorating: assorted sprinkles

My favourite recipe headnote comes from cookbook queen Nigella Lawson's *Nigella Bites*. Writing about her chocolate fudge cake, she claims that it's the kind of thing you'd want to eat in its entirety when you've been dumped as just the sight of it offers immense comfort. She then states it can serve 10 or "1 with a broken heart." I can't imagine conveying the responsibility of a good chocolate cake any more clearly.

1. Preheat the oven to 350°F (180°C). Lightly grease a 9- × 13-inch (23 × 33 cm) baking pan. Line the bottom of the pan with parchment paper. Do not let the parchment paper hang over the sides of the pan if you plan to serve the cake directly from the pan. Set aside.

2. To make the cake, in a medium mixing bowl, stir together the flour, cocoa powder, sugar, baking powder, baking soda, and salt. Pour in the melted butter, oil, eggs, coffee, buttermilk, and vanilla and whisk until the batter is smooth.

3. Pour the batter into the prepared pan and bake until the cake is firm to the touch, 30 to 35 minutes. Remove the pan from the oven, transfer to a wire rack, and let cool completely. Once the cake is cool, you can remove it from the pan by running a knife around the perimeter to loosen the edges, and then invert it onto your work surface. I also highly recommend just leaving the cake in the pan and serving it directly from there, which is what I always do.

4. To make the frosting, in a microwave-safe mixing bowl, melt the chocolate chips as follows. Heat in the microwave on medium-high for 1 minute. Remove from the microwave and stir. Repeat heating at 15- to 20-second intervals, stirring in between, until the mixture is completely melted and smooth.

5. Whisk in the sour cream and vanilla, beating until silky smooth. The frosting should be thick enough to spread over the cake, but if not, refrigerate until it cools (it will thicken as it cools).

6. Using a small offset spatula, spread the frosting over the top of the cake. There will be enough frosting to cover the top and sides of the cake, should you choose to remove it from the baking pan. Don't fret about making the icing too perfect—you're going for a rustic look.

7. Decorate the cake with sprinkles, if using, and let sit for at least 1 hour before serving, so the frosting can firm up. Cut into squares and serve.

FOUR SEASON FRUIT CRISP

VEGETARIAN, MAKE AHEAD, KID FRIENDLY

Each crisp serves 6

Crisps and cobblers are quite popular in the fall, but I think they're perfect anytime of the year. There's always some fruit available to turn into this simple, classic dessert, even in March when strawberry season seems impossibly far away. I have a variation for each season and use *almost* the same topping for all of them, save for the nuts, which I swap according to which fruit is in season. You'll notice I call for a range of cornstarch to be used in the fillings. Less leaky fruits will only require 2 tablespoons, while juicier fruits (berries, I'm looking at you!) will use all 4 tablespoons.

TOPPING

1. In a medium mixing bowl, stir together the flour, oats, sugar, nuts, cinnamon, salt, and butter. Chill in the refrigerator until ready to use.

FALL FRUIT CRISP

1. Preheat the oven to 375°F (190°C).
2. Place the apple and plum slices in an ungreased 8- × 8-inch (20 × 20 cm) casserole dish. Add the lemon juice, sugar, cinnamon, cornstarch, and salt and gently toss with a large spoon to combine. Scatter the prepared topping over the fruit.
3. Bake until the fruit is bubbly and the topping is golden brown, 25 to 35 minutes. Serve warm or at room temperature with vanilla ice cream, if using. It's highly recommended.

WINTER FRUIT CRISP

1. Preheat the oven to 375°F (190°C).
2. Place the pear slices and cranberries in an ungreased 2-quart (1.9 L) or similar-size casserole dish. Add the orange juice, sugar, cinnamon, cornstarch, and salt and gently toss with a large spoon to combine. Scatter the prepared topping over the fruit.
3. Bake until the fruit is bubbly and the topping is golden brown, 25 to 35 minutes. Serve warm or at room temperature with vanilla ice cream, if using. It's highly recommended.

Recipe continues . . .

For the topping

½ cup (125 mL) all-purpose flour

½ cup (125 mL) old-fashioned rolled oats

½ cup (125 mL) cane or brown sugar

¼ cup (60 mL) chopped nuts (see seasonal recipes for suggested nut)

½ teaspoon (2 mL) cinnamon

Pinch of salt

⅓ cup (85 mL) butter, melted

For the fall fruit crisp

Use walnuts in the crisp topping

3 cups (750 mL) peeled, cored, and sliced (½ inch/1 cm thick) apples (assorted varieties)

3 cups (750 mL) pitted and sliced (½ inch/1 cm thick) plums

2 tablespoons (30 mL) fresh lemon juice

2 tablespoons (30 mL) brown sugar

1 teaspoon (5 mL) ground cinnamon

2 to 4 tablespoons (30 to 60 mL) cornstarch

Pinch of kosher salt

Vanilla ice cream (optional)

For the winter fruit crisp

Use pecans in the crisp topping

4 cups (1 L) peeled, cored, and sliced (½ inch/1 cm thick) pears

2 cups (500 mL) fresh or frozen cranberries

2 tablespoons (30 mL) freshly squeezed orange juice

2 tablespoons (30 mL) brown sugar

1 teaspoon (5 mL) ground cinnamon

2 to 4 tablespoons (30 to 60 mL) cornstarch

Pinch of kosher salt

Vanilla ice cream (optional)

For the spring fruit crisp

Use pistachios in the crisp topping

4 cups (1 L) hulled and halved
   strawberries

2 cups (500 mL) trimmed and chopped
   (1 inch/2.5 cm thick) rhubarb

1 tablespoon (15 mL) fresh lemon juice

½ cup (125 mL) cane sugar

1 teaspoon (5 mL) pure vanilla extract

2 to 4 tablespoons (30 to 60 mL)
   cornstarch

Pinch of kosher salt

Vanilla ice cream (optional)

For the summer fruit crisp

Use almonds in the crisp topping

4 cups (1 L) pitted, cored, and sliced
   (½ inch/1 cm thick) stone fruit (any
   kind)

2 cups (500 mL) fresh blueberries

2 tablespoons (30 mL) fresh lemon
   juice

2 tablespoons (30 mL) brown sugar

1 teaspoon (5 mL) ground cinnamon

2 to 4 tablespoons (30 to 60 mL)
   cornstarch

Pinch of kosher salt

Vanilla ice cream (optional)

SPRING FRUIT CRISP

1. Preheat the oven to 375°F (190°C).
2. Place the strawberries and rhubarb in an ungreased 2-quart (1.9 L) or similar-size casserole dish. Add the lemon juice, sugar, vanilla, cornstarch, and salt and gently toss with a large spoon to combine. Scatter the prepared topping over the fruit.
3. Bake until the fruit is bubbly and the topping is golden brown, 25 to 35 minutes. Serve warm or at room temperature with vanilla ice cream, if using. It's highly recommended.

SUMMER FRUIT CRISP

1. Preheat the oven to 375°F (190°C).
2. Place the stone fruit slices and blueberries in an ungreased 2-quart (1.9 L) or similar-size casserole dish. Add the lemon juice, sugar, cinnamon, cornstarch, and salt and gently toss with a large spoon to combine. Scatter the prepared topping over the fruit.
3. Bake until the fruit is bubbly and the topping is golden brown, 25 to 35 minutes. Serve warm or at room temperature with vanilla ice cream, if using. It's highly recommended.

TRIPLE BERRY CRUMB BARS

VEGETARIAN, MAKE AHEAD, KID FRIENDLY

Makes 16 bars

Handheld snacks are ideal for warm-weather eating; they're casual, easy to tote around, and require nothing more than your fingers for easy consumption. These crumb bars fit the bill perfectly, and in addition to their simplicity, they're also not too sweet. They are completely customizable and work with whatever berry is in season, even though I'm partial to using three berries together. Here's another bonus for the warm-weather months: these treats travel well (think potlucks, picnics, and road trip snacks) and make just enough to feed a large group without too many leftovers.

½ cup (125 mL) butter, room temperature, plus extra for pan

6 tablespoons (90 mL) butter, melted

½ cup (125 mL) packed brown sugar

1½ cups (375 mL) all-purpose flour, divided

½ teaspoon (2 mL) salt, divided

1 cup (250 mL) powdered sugar

1 teaspoon (5 mL) vanilla bean paste or pure vanilla extract

2 large eggs

½ teaspoon (2 mL) baking powder

1 cup (250 mL) fresh blueberries

½ cup (125 mL) fresh raspberries

½ cup (125 mL) fresh blackberries

1. Preheat the oven to 350°F (180°C). Butter an 8-inch (20 cm) square baking pan and line the bottom with parchment paper, leaving a 2-inch (5 cm) overhang on 2 sides.

2. To make the crumb topping, in a medium bowl, combine the melted butter, brown sugar, ¾ cup (175 mL) flour, and ¼ teaspoon (1 mL) salt. Mix with a fork until moist and crumbly. Cover and place in the refrigerator until ready to use.

3. In the bowl of an electric mixer, beat the ½ cup (125 mL) room-temperature butter, powdered sugar, and vanilla until light and fluffy.

4. Add the eggs, one at a time, beating well after each addition. Add the remaining ¾ cup (175 mL) flour, the remaining ¼ teaspoon (1 mL) salt, and the baking powder to the bowl. With the mixer on low, beat until just combined.

5. Spread the batter evenly over the bottom of the prepared pan. Sprinkle with the berries and cover with the chilled crumb topping. Bake until golden brown and a toothpick inserted into the centre comes out with no crumbs attached, about 35 to 40 minutes.

6. Remove the pan from the oven and let cool completely. Lift out the bars using the paper overhang. Cut into 16 squares and store in an airtight container in the refrigerator for up to 5 days or in the freezer for up to 2 months.

Serves 6 to 8

12 sugar cones, broken into large
pieces
½ cup (125 mL) chopped pecans
½ cup (125 mL) unsweetened flaked
coconut
2 tablespoons (30 mL) cane or
granulated sugar
½ cup (125 mL) unsalted butter, melted
Pinch of salt
4 cups (1 L) ice cream, any flavour
Optional toppings for serving: drizzled
melted chocolate, whipped cream,
chocolate sauce, crushed sugar
cones

ICE CREAM CONE PIE

Unlike almost 80 percent of the recipes in this book, this ice cream pie is one I created specifically for summer. My fourth favourite season of the year, the months between June and September tend to drag on a little too long for me, and by the time we reach August I find myself as emotionally wilted as the ferns on my front porch. To boost my spirits, I usually turn to food for comfort, and this is what I crave when the days are endlessly hot and humid. It's simple to make, takes very little time in the oven, and impresses almost all who encounter it. I like to use two flavours of ice cream in this pie, but you can use a single flavour if you prefer. Be sure to serve this pie with a spoonful of whipped cream and a generous drizzle of chocolate sauce if you have them around. Oh, and for those who truly love summer, this dessert is perfect for warm-weather birthdays, backyard barbecues, and anytime you feel like celebrating the season.

1. Preheat the oven to 375° (190°C). In the bowl of a food processor fitted with a steel blade, process the ice cream cones into a fine crumb. Add the pecans, coconut, sugar, butter, and salt and pulse until the mixture resembles wet sand.

2. Press the mixture into a 9-inch (23 cm) pie plate, patting it into the bottom and up the sides of the pan. Bake for 8 to 10 minutes or until the crust is golden brown.

3. Remove the pie plate from the oven and let cool completely. While the pie crust cools, take the ice cream out of the freezer and let it come to room temperature on the counter.

4. Spoon the ice cream into the pie crust. I like to use two different flavours, dropping dollops of both haphazardly over the crust. Using an offset spatula, swirl the ice cream into an even layer. Cover with plastic wrap and freeze for 4 to 6 hours or until the ice cream has hardened.

5. Remove the pie from the freezer and let sit at room temperature for 15 to 20 minutes. Slice the pie into wedges and top with whipped cream, chocolate sauce, and crushed sugar cones, if using. Leftover pie can be stored, covered with plastic wrap, in the pan in the freezer for 5 days.

INDIVIDUAL MOCHA MOLTEN CAKES

VEGETARIAN, MAKE AHEAD, KID FRIENDLY

Makes 12 individual cakes

With their tender brownie-like crusts and creamy pudding-like centres that ooze when you cut into them, you can serve these supremely rich cakes on their own or topped with whipped cream or ice cream. Surprisingly easy to make, they taste like you've spent hours in the kitchen perfecting the recipe. As with all good and essential recipes, you can make these ahead of when you need to bake them. To do so, make the batter, fill the muffin cups, and refrigerate or freeze; they can go straight into the oven from either. Keep in mind that they may need a minute or two more cooking time if baking from frozen.

1. Preheat the oven to 325°F (160°C). Grease a standard 12-cup muffin tin with non-stick spray or line with paper liners and set aside.
2. In a medium bowl, melt the chocolate and butter in the microwave on medium-high in 20-second increments, stirring in between, until the chocolate is completely smooth. Stir in the espresso powder.
3. In a second bowl, using a whisk, beat the eggs and sugar until light and fluffy, about 1 minute. Add the flour, baking powder, salt, and melted chocolate mixture. Carefully mix with a rubber spatula or wooden spoon until just combined.
4. Divide the batter evenly between the muffin cups, and bake until the cakes have just cooked through and the tops are semi-matte, 10 to 12 minutes. The cakes will look a little moist on top, which is what you want.
5. Remove the muffin tin from the oven and let cool for 5 to 10 minutes. Run a knife around the rim of each muffin cup and carefully remove the cakes from the pan. Serve warm with ice cream and caramel sauce, if using.

10 ounces (300 g) semi-sweet or bittersweet chocolate, chopped
4 tablespoons (60 mL) unsalted butter
¾ teaspoon (4 mL) espresso powder
4 large eggs
½ cup (125 mL) granulated sugar
½ cup + 2 tablespoons (155 mL) all-purpose flour
½ teaspoon (2 mL) baking powder
¼ teaspoon (1 mL) kosher salt
Optional toppings for serving: ice cream, caramel sauce

TIP: These cakes are best eaten shortly after they are baked. The molten centres will firm up as they continue to cool. Having said that, they will still taste delicious, just not be nearly as gooey as when they first came out of the oven.

BAKING PAN 101: THE PRACTICAL KITCHEN COMPANION

Successful baking requires creativity, carefully selected ingredients, and a lot of love—something I'd argue is essential to turning out tasty treats. Although these three things are key, they won't work their magic without the use of the right baking pan. Often referred to as a baking *dish* (they are not the same), for our purposes a baking *pan* refers to a metal pan—usually steel or aluminized steel and often with a non-stick coating—ideal for making baked goods like bars, cookies, sheet cakes, muffins, and savoury creations such as the Spinach and Ricotta Wonton Mini Lasagnas (page 159) and Muffin Pan Tuna Melts (page 107).

WHAT TO LOOK FOR

Invest in good quality, heavy-duty pans that are known to retain heat well. You also want to avoid pans that buckle or warp easily. Most pans are available in a light or dark finish and often have curved corners, but if you can find pans with straight, 90-degree corners, snatch them up because the finished product always yields more defined, professional-looking baking. Although there are several commonly used types of baking pans, the ones that tend to get the most use are 8-inch (20 cm) square pans, 9-inch (23 cm) square pans, round cake pans, muffin tins, loaf pans, springform pans, and pie plates.

SQUARE BAKING PANS: You can usually find these in an 8-inch (20 cm) version, but a 9-inch (23 cm) square pan can work just as easily. Most commonly used for bars, brownies, and some cakes, pans should be at least 2 inches (5 cm) deep to avoid overflow of batter. You can use these pans interchangeably, but just know that if the recipe calls for an 8-inch (20 cm) pan and you use a 9-inch (23 cm) pan instead, the bars or cake will bake faster because the batter is spread over a larger pan (the reverse is true as well!). I recommend owning a pan of each size.

ROUND CAKE PANS: Essentially the same as square baking pans, these are most frequently used for cakes and are available in many sizes. The most commonly used sizes are 6 inches (15 cm), 8 inches (20 cm), 9 inches (23 cm), and 10 inches (25 cm). Start by purchasing either two 8-inch (20 cm) or two 9-inch (23 cm) pans (many cake recipes involve two layers, so you'll need two pans) and then add to your collection as needed.

MUFFIN TINS: Available in three different sizes—6-cup jumbo, 12-cup standard, or 24-cup mini—muffin tins are used to bake muffins and cupcakes as well as single servings of savoury foods like lasagna (page 159). Traditionally made of metal (though flexible silicone pans are now available), each cup in a standard 12-cup muffin tin is 2½ to 2¾ inches (6 to 7 cm) in diameter. Start by owning one standard 12-cup muffin tin and then add to your collection as you see fit.

LOAF PANS: Most of us already have a loaf pan tucked away, and therefore are past the point of purchasing a new one, but if you do need to add one of these to your kitchen, know that they come in a variety of shapes and sizes, not to mention materials. There are metal pans—both non-stick and stainless steel or aluminum—glass pans, ceramic pans, and silicone pans.

Metal loaf pans are wonderful for browning the edges of breads, while ceramic loaf pans have the benefit of doubling as an attractive serving dish. The most useful size falls somewhere between 8½ × 4½ inches (21 × 11 cm) and 9 × 5 inches (23 × 13 cm). Start with a standard-size metal pan and add a ceramic one to your arsenal if you choose to expand your collection.

SPRINGFORM PANS: These pans are most often used for cheesecake or other delicate cakes that would be damaged by turning them upside down to remove them from the pan, but I'm partial to using them to make my Simple Meat-Lover's Deep-Dish Pizza (page 109). They are sturdy and round, and fitted with expandable sides that are secured with a clamp. The removable bottom is easily released when the clamp is opened. Look for pans where the bottom is tightly locked into the sides when the clamp is sealed, otherwise the pan will leak. You will probably only ever need to buy one of these in your lifetime (unless the clamp breaks); look for one that is 9 to 10 inches (23 to 25 cm) in diameter.

PIE PLATES: I prefer to use glass pie plates, as they allow the crust to colour well and the transparency of the glass allows me to keep an eye on how the crust is browning. The exception to this is when I make a slab pie (page 215); I always use a rimmed sheet pan instead. Ceramic and stoneware pie plates look lovely on the table and can be purchased inexpensively in a variety of colours to suit any holiday theme or special occasion. Metal pie plates are more durable than glass or ceramic but don't look as nice, and dark metal pans can cause overbrowning. I like pie plates that are 9 inches (23 cm) in diameter, but some of the newer pans are deep and closer to 10 inches

(25 cm); pay close attention to the size of the pan when you are purchasing to be sure you get the right size for you.

CARING FOR AND CLEANING BAKING PANS

Completely cool metal and non-stick baking pans before washing them, and keep in mind that most should be handwashed in warm, soapy water. Avoid abrasive scrubbers and clean the inner corners thoroughly so that no food or grease is left behind. Thoroughly dry your pans before storing them in the cupboard. To minimize cleanup, you can line muffin tins with paper or silicone liners and other baking pans with parchment paper or aluminum foil.

HOW TO STORE

The most challenging thing about storing baking pans is finding room for them! Durable and sturdy, they stack well and can fit snugly against each other without worrying about scratching fragile surfaces, but regardless of their resilience, you still need a place to put them. Although cupboards are the natural choice, some homes don't have the extra space. I keep my essential pans in my kitchen and store the overflow in my basement. You could also consider stashing your pans on top of your kitchen cabinets, in that vacant space between the cabinets and the ceiling.

TOP TIPS FOR USE

- Prepare your pan before baking so that the batter can be poured into the pan as soon as it's ready.
- If using dark metal or glass baking pans, you may want to reduce the oven temperature by 25°F (10°C).
- Always try to use the pan size specified in the recipe; however, substitutions can be made if necessary.

SAUCES, SNACKS, AND SIPS

BENJAMIN FRANKLIN FAMOUSLY once said, "A place for everything and everything in its place." It would be nice to apply that principle to cookbooks, but sometimes there are recipes that don't fit neatly into a specific chapter but are worthy of inclusion regardless of being a little homeless. This chapter is dedicated to such dishes. It's where to turn when you're feeling peckish or craving the comforts of a warming drink (with minimal effort required!) like Rich Hot Chocolate (page 258), which my kids are always craving. You'll find pantry staples—my refrigerator is never without a jar of Quick Pickled Jalapeños (page 248) or Berry Chia Jam (page 250)—and simple sauces that will make some of the book's recipes shine. Like the rest of the recipes in this book, they are made in one pan, pot, or skillet, also allowing you to create crave-worthy party snacks. The Roasted Red Onion Party Dip (page 239) is my go-to easy entertaining appetizer, but when I'm looking to serve something a little more sophisticated I turn to the Mixed Olives with Chorizo and Almonds (page 242).

WARM ARTICHOKE, KALE, AND WHITE BEAN DIP

VEGETARIAN, MAKE AHEAD, KID FRIENDLY, QUICK COOKING, GLUTEN-FREE

Serves 6 to 10, or a medium-size crowd

½ cup (125 mL) cream cheese

½ cup (125 mL) good quality mayonnaise

½ cup (125 mL) sour cream

1 can (19 ounces/540 mL) white beans (navy or cannellini), drained and rinsed

1 jar (6 ounces/170 mL) marinated artichoke hearts, drained and chopped

1 package (10 ounces/300 g) frozen chopped kale, thawed, drained, and squeezed dry

2 cloves garlic, grated or pressed

Few dashes of hot sauce

1 cup (250 mL) grated mozzarella cheese, divided

½ cup (125 mL) grated Parmesan cheese, divided

Tortilla chips, for serving

This is everything I believe a hot dip should be: warm and cheesy. It's a crowd-pleaser and can be made ahead of time and frozen until needed, something I almost always do during the hectic holiday season. Feel free to replace the kale with a standard package of frozen chopped spinach if that's easier for you to find. I touch on the topic of good quality mayonnaise on page 239.

1. Preheat the oven to 350°F (180°C). Lightly grease an 8- × 8-inch (20 × 20 cm) casserole dish and set aside.

2. In the bowl of a food processor fitted with a steel blade, add the cream cheese, mayonnaise, sour cream, and beans and process until smooth. Add the artichokes and pulse until the dip is smooth with a few chunks remaining.

3. Spoon the mixture into a medium bowl and stir in the kale, garlic, and hot sauce. Add half each of the mozzarella and Parmesan and mix well to combine.

4. Tip the mixture into the prepared dish and cover with the remaining mozzarella and Parmesan. Bake for 20 to 25 minutes or until bubbly and brown. Serve warm with tortilla chips.

TIP: The dip can be made through step 4 and then, instead of being baked, can be covered tightly with plastic wrap and frozen for up to 2 months. When you're ready to serve it, remove the dish from the freezer, uncover, and place it in the oven while it preheats. Then bake as per the recipe instructions, adding an extra 5 to 10 minutes if needed.

ROASTED RED ONION PARTY DIP

Serves 6 to 10, or a medium-size crowd

This dip is designed to feed a crowd, and I make it for most birthday parties and holiday gatherings. I tend to take turns serving it with kettle chips, assorted vegetables, or crackers, but sometimes I go wild and put all three on a plate. This dip will convince you that there's no longer any need to buy a store-bought variety. This dish relies heavily on a good amount of mayonnaise, and although it's hard to beat the flavour of a homemade mayo, when you're in need of a large quantity, a store-bought variety is the way to go. I call for a good quality mayonnaise, and by that I mean the brand with the most straightforward list of ingredients. Fewer fillers and additives will result in a better tasting product, so keep that in mind when you're making your purchase. On the topic of mayonnaise, be sure that is indeed what you purchase, and not its sweeter and spicier cousin most commonly referred to as "dressing."

2 large red onions

2 tablespoons (30 mL) olive oil

1½ teaspoons (7 mL) kosher salt

¼ teaspoon (1 mL) cayenne pepper

8 ounces (225 g) cream cheese, softened

1 cup (250 mL) sour cream

1 cup (250 mL) good quality mayonnaise

Chopped fresh chives, for garnish

1. Preheat the oven to 425°F (220°C).
2. Using a sharp knife, trims the ends from each onion and slice in half lengthwise. Then cut each half lengthwise into quarters.
3. On a sheet pan, scatter the onion pieces and drizzle with the oil. Sprinkle with the salt and cayenne and toss with your fingers to evenly combine.
4. Roast for 25 to 35 minutes, stirring once halfway through cooking, or until the onion pieces are soft and the tips are golden brown. Remove the sheet pan from the oven and let cool completely.
5. Into the bowl of a food processor fitted with a steel blade, scoop the cream cheese, sour cream, and mayonnaise. Process until smooth. Scrape the onions and oil from the sheet pan into the bowl of the food processor, and pulse until finely chopped and well combined.
6. Check seasonings and add more salt if needed. Scrape the dip into a bowl, cover, and chill for at least 4 hours. Let sit at room temperature for 1 hour before serving. Garnish with chives, if using.

TIP: You can make this dip up to 3 days before serving.

BUFFALO CHICKEN AND BLUE CHEESE–STUFFED CELERY STICKS

Makes about 30 sticks

¼ cup (60 mL) hot sauce, such as
   Frank's RedHot Sauce

3 tablespoons (45 mL) butter, melted

2 teaspoons (10 mL) brown sugar

1 teaspoon (5 mL) smoked paprika

½ teaspoon (2 mL) salt

2 cups (500 mL) shredded, cooked
   chicken

1 bunch celery

½ cup (125 mL) crumbled blue cheese

I like to think of these as a mess-free and calorie-conscious alternative to traditional chicken wings. Although this recipe makes enough to feed a medium-size crowd, if you've got a group of guys over to watch hockey or football, you may want to consider preparing a double batch.

1. Position a rack in the top third of the oven and preheat to broil. Lightly grease an 8- × 8-inch (20 × 20 cm) casserole dish and set aside.

2. In a medium bowl, whisk together the hot sauce, butter, brown sugar, paprika, and salt. Add the shredded chicken and toss to coat.

3. Tip the chicken mixture into the prepared casserole dish and bake until crispy and caramelized on top, 3 to 4 minutes. Remove the casserole dish from the oven and let cool for 1 to 2 minutes.

4. Meanwhile, cut each celery stalk into 3 even pieces.

5. Stuff each celery piece with 2 to 3 tablespoons (30 to 45 mL) of the chicken mixture and top with some blue cheese. Serve immediately.

BAKED MOZZARELLA STICKS

VEGETARIAN, MAKE AHEAD, KID FRIENDLY, QUICK COOKING

Makes 24 sticks; serves 4 to 8

What I like most about these cheesy snacks is that they're baked, not fried, yet just as delicious. There is no denying that they're a favourite in our home, and they're just as well received when served as an after-school snack as when they appear on the appetizer table at a birthday party or family get-together.

1. Place the flour on a wide, shallow plate. Crack the eggs into the middle of a second wide, shallow plate and beat with a fork until blended. On a third similar-size plate, combine the panko, Parmesan, parsley, and garlic powder. Season to taste with pepper and stir well.

2. Line a small rimmed sheet pan with parchment paper. One at a time, lightly roll the cheese sticks in the flour, shaking off any excess, then dip in the egg, and finally in the seasoned panko. Re-dip each stick in the egg, and then in the panko mixture, and place on the prepared pan. Freeze for at least 30 minutes.

3. When ready to bake, position a rack in the bottom third of the oven and heat the oven to 400°F (200°C). Remove the sheet pan from the freezer and drizzle the oil over the cheese sticks. Turn to coat.

4. Bake for 4 to 5 minutes, then flip the cheese sticks over and bake for another 4 to 5 minutes or until the panko is golden and the cheese is soft. Meanwhile, warm the tomato sauce in the microwave. Arrange the mozzarella sticks on a platter and serve with warm tomato sauce on the side.

¼ cup (60 mL) all-purpose flour

3 large eggs

1 cup (250 mL) panko bread crumbs

1 tablespoon (15 mL) freshly grated Parmesan cheese

1 tablespoon (15 mL) finely chopped fresh parsley

¼ teaspoon (1 mL) garlic powder

Freshly ground black pepper

12 partly skimmed mozzarella string cheese sticks, unwrapped and cut in half

1 tablespoon (15 mL) olive oil

1 cup (250 mL) Roasted Tomato Sauce (page 244) or store-bought tomato sauce

TIP: Regular mozzarella cheese cut into 4- × ½-inch (10 × 1 cm) pieces can be substituted for the string cheese. Don't be alarmed if the cheese sticks flatten as they bake.

MIXED OLIVES WITH CHORIZO AND ALMONDS

Serves 4 to 6 as an appetizer

3 tablespoons (45 mL) extra-virgin olive oil, divided

4 ounces (110 g) chorizo (or similar smoked sausage), sliced into ½-inch (1 cm) thick half moons

1 teaspoon (5 mL) crushed red pepper flakes

2 cloves garlic, thinly sliced

2 strips orange peel, each 2 × ½ inches (5 × 1 cm)

1 tablespoon (15 mL) fresh sage leaves, thinly sliced

1 cup (250 mL) unpitted large black olives

1 cup (250 mL) unpitted large green olives

1 cup (250 mL) Marcona almonds

Crusty bread, sliced, for serving

Warm skillet olives are one of the easiest appetizers a home cook can make, yet they're impressive enough to convince your guests you secretly moonlight as a private chef. The combination of ingredients is as simple as it is sophisticated, yet this dish is versatile when your taste buds want to travel from Spain to Italy, or even to France. This version definitely boasts the flavours of Spain, but you could just as easily make it Italian by swapping the chorizo for chopped salami and the sage for fresh rosemary. If it's France your taste buds want to travel to, skip the meat altogether and add a few bay leaves and ½ teaspoon (2 mL) fennel seed to the skillet. Marcona almonds—blanched, peeled almonds fried in olive oil and seasoned with salt—are available in finer grocery stores or bulk food stores, but if you can't find them, you can replace them with regular roasted almonds.

1. In a medium cast iron, stainless steel, or non-stick skillet, warm 1 tablespoon (15 mL) oil over medium heat. Add the chorizo and cook for 3 minutes or until it begins to crisp. Transfer to a plate lined with paper towel and set aside.

2. Drizzle the remaining 2 tablespoons (30 mL) oil into the skillet. Add the red pepper flakes, garlic, orange peel, and sage and cook, stirring occasionally, until the oil is infused and fragrant, 2 to 3 minutes.

3. Add the olives and almonds. Cook, stirring every few minutes, until warmed through, 3 to 5 minutes. Return the chorizo to the skillet and cook for 1 minute more. Serve at once with slices of crusty bread for mopping up the oil.

ROASTED TOMATO SAUCE

VEGETARIAN, MAKE AHEAD,
KID FRIENDLY, GLUTEN-FREE

Makes 5 to 6 cups (1.25 to 1.5 L)

2 cans (28 ounces/796 mL each) whole
    peeled tomatoes

8 cloves garlic, peeled and crushed

1 small onion, peeled and finely
    chopped

½ teaspoon (2 mL) granulated sugar

1½ teaspoons (7 mL) kosher salt

2 tablespoons (30 mL) tomato paste

¼ cup (60 mL) unsalted butter, cut into
    small pieces

½ teaspoon (2 mL) crushed red pepper
    flakes

1 teaspoon (5 mL) dried basil

1 teaspoon (5 mL) dried oregano

I've already mentioned a few times how much I dislike tomatoes, but I do recognize that they have a place in my diet, namely in sauces. This tomato sauce is a good example of when I will eat tomatoes. I love when they're cooked down with aromatics and seasonings and simmered until they become soft and jammy. I'm sure that tomato lovers and tomato haters alike will agree this is a fine way to enjoy them. Use this sauce anytime tomato or marinara sauce is called for in a recipe.

1. Preheat the oven to 425°F (220°C).
2. Using your hands, crush the tomatoes into a 9- × 13-inch (23 × 33 cm) enamel roasting pan. If you don't want to get your fingers dirty, you can use a pair of scissors to roughly chop the tomatoes in the can before adding them to the pan.
3. Add the garlic, onion, sugar, salt, tomato paste, butter, red pepper flakes, basil, and oregano, and stir to combine. Roast, tossing halfway through, until tomatoes and garlic are soft and the sauce looks jammy, 45 to 50 minutes.
4. Remove the pan from the oven and let cool for a minimum of 5 minutes, then transfer the sauce to the carafe of a blender and blend until it reaches the desired consistency. For a chunkier sauce, pulse just a few times; for one that's smoother, let the motor run until the sauce is perfectly puréed. Store in a jar in the refrigerator for up to 5 days or in 3- to 4-cup (750 mL to 1 L) portions in the freezer for up to 3 months.

PANTRY PIZZA SAUCE

VEGETARIAN, MAKE AHEAD, KID FRIENDLY,
QUICK COOKING, GLUTEN-FREE

Makes about 3 cups (750 mL)

Canned and jarred pizza sauces are readily available in almost every grocery store, and you can certainly use those options if you prefer. However, once you try this super-simple recipe, I'm certain you'll become a convert to the homemade variety. I like to use this sauce when I make Salami Stromboli (page 110), Simple Meat-Lover's Deep-Dish Pizza (page 109), or a Personal Pan-Fried Pizza (page 100). It literally takes minutes to prepare, and then patiently simmers on the stove while you prep your pizza ingredients. This can be made several days in advance if you prefer and will keep well in the freezer for a few months.

1 small onion, peeled and roughly chopped
2 cloves garlic
2 tablespoons (30 mL) olive oil
1 can (28 ounces/796 mL) crushed tomatoes
½ to 1 teaspoon (2 to 5 mL) granulated sugar
1½ teaspoons (7 mL) kosher salt
1 teaspoon (5 mL) dried oregano
Pinch of crushed red pepper flakes

1. In a medium Dutch oven (4 to 6 quarts/3.8 to 5.7 L), sauté the onion and garlic in the oil over medium heat until soft and fragrant, about 3 to 4 minutes.

2. Reduce the heat to medium-low and add the tomatoes, ½ teaspoon (2 mL) sugar, salt, oregano, and red pepper flakes. Simmer, uncovered, for 20 to 30 minutes, keeping the heat low enough that the sauce barely bubbles.

3. Remove the Dutch oven from the stovetop and let cool for a minimum of 5 minutes. Transfer the sauce to the carafe of a blender or the bowl of a food processor fitted with a steel blade and process until smooth. If the sauce tastes too acidic, add more sugar. Store in a covered air-tight container in the fridge for up to 5 days or in 3- to 4-cup (750 mL to 1L) portions in the freezer for up to 3 months.

TIP: If you have fresh basil on hand, stir a few chopped leaves into the sauce as it simmers.

QUICK PICKLED JALAPEÑOS

VEGETARIAN, MAKE AHEAD,
QUICK COOKING, GLUTEN-FREE

Makes about 4 cups (1 L)

1 cup (250 mL) white vinegar

1 cup (250 mL) water

3 tablespoons (45 mL) cane sugar

2 cloves garlic, grated or pressed

2 teaspoons (10 mL) kosher salt

1 teaspoon (5 mL) dried oregano

10 jalapeño peppers, trimmed and
    thinly sliced

This condiment is essential for summer, and we're rarely without a jar in our fridge. My husband spoons these over his Turkey Lentil Sloppy Joes (page 113), and a jar can always be found resting beside a pot of my Perfect Saucy Pulled Pork (page 134). Don't hesitate to spoon them over the Chili-Lime Potato Nachos (page 151), and you can even slip a few into the Crispy Black Bean Tacos (page 152) if you aren't afraid of a little heat. Use them to top nachos, tacos, sandwiches, salads, and burgers, or stir them into a breakfast dish like the Spicy Corn and Bacon Frittata (page 21).

1. In a medium Dutch oven (4 to 6 quarts/3.8 to 5.7 L), combine the vinegar, water, sugar, garlic, salt, and oregano and bring to a boil over high heat.
2. Add the jalapeños, stir once, and remove from the heat. Let steep for 12 minutes.
3. Using tongs, transfer the peppers to a glass jar; pour the brining liquid into the container, covering the jalapeños completely. Cover and refrigerate until needed. These will keep in the refrigerator for up to 1 month.

BERRY CHIA JAM

VEGETARIAN, MAKE AHEAD, KID FRIENDLY, QUICK COOKING, GLUTEN-FREE

Makes about 2 cups (500 mL)

1 pound (450 g) berries (I like raspberries best), frozen and unthawed or fresh

1½ tablespoons (22 mL) fresh lemon juice

2 tablespoons (30 mL) liquid honey

2 tablespoons (30 mL) chia seeds

½ teaspoon (2 mL) vanilla bean paste or pure vanilla extract

I've been making a batch of this jam every other week since the summer of 2015, when my youngest son started eating solid foods. When the chia seeds come into contact with the berries, the liquid gives them a thick, jelly-like consistency, removing the need for pectin and pounds of sugar. We spoon this jam over oatmeal, smear it on thick-cut slices of toast, dollop it on Our Favourite Pancakes (page 34), bake it into our beloved Almond Butter and Jam Breakfast Bars (page 43), and even stir it into yogurt along with a sprinkling of Golden Apricot Granola (page 36).

1. In a medium Dutch oven (4 to 6 quarts/3.8 to 5.7 L), bring the berries and lemon juice to a boil over medium-high heat, stirring frequently. Reduce heat to low, and simmer until the berries soften, about 5 minutes.
2. Mash the berries with the back of a fork. Stir in the honey and chia seeds. Cook until the jam thickens, 5 to 7 minutes, stirring frequently to ensure it doesn't stick to the bottom of the pot.
3. Remove the Dutch oven from the heat and stir in the vanilla. Allow to cool to room temperature (the jam will thicken as it cools). Transfer to a covered container and store in the refrigerator for up to 2 weeks.

TIP: This jam can be frozen in a freezer-safe container for up to 3 months.

TOASTED NUTS, TWO WAYS

VEGETARIAN, MAKE AHEAD, GLUTEN-FREE

In most cases, toasting nuts improves both the flavour and the texture of a dish. It brings their oils to the surface, creating a richer colour while also intensifying the flavour and making them crunchier. Toasted walnuts bring some needed crunch to the Roasted Lentil and Walnut Salad with Grapes, Spinach, and Goat Cheese (page 182) and help to make the Maple Walnut Biscotti (page 205) shine. The oven is ideal for large batches of nuts, while a skillet is an easy way to toast a smaller amount. It should be noted that using a skillet requires a little more attention, as it's easier for the nuts to burn. Smaller nuts, such as pine nuts, will take less time to toast than larger varieties, such as pecans or walnuts. Lastly, keep in mind that it's best to toast nuts whole and then chop them afterwards if necessary.

THE OVEN METHOD

1. Preheat the oven to 350°F (180°C) and line a rimmed sheet pan with parchment paper. Place the nuts on the sheet pan in a single layer and bake for 5 to 10 minutes or until golden brown and fragrant. The timing will vary depending on the nut you're toasting. You'll know they are done when their fragrance and colour change.
2. Remove the sheet pan from the oven, transfer the nuts to a plate, and let cool completely. Store any extra toasted nuts in an airtight container in the freezer for 1 to 3 months.

THE SKILLET METHOD

1. In a dry cast iron or stainless steel skillet, toast the nuts in a single layer over medium heat for 2 to 3 minutes or until their colour begins to change. Toss them to flip over, and repeat on the other side. Watch them closely, as it's easy to burn them at this stage. You'll know they are done when their fragrance and colour change.
2. Transfer the nuts to a plate and let cool completely. Store any extra toasted nuts in an airtight container in the freezer for 1 to 3 months.

TIP: Take note if you love to bake. Toasted nuts are less likely to sink in a cake and are easier to chop when they are warm.

Makes 3 to 4 cups (750 mL to 1 L)

For the oven method

3 to 4 cups (750 mL to 1 L) nuts,
 any kind

Makes 1 to 2 cups (250 to 500 mL)

For the skillet method

1 to 2 cups (250 to 500 mL) nuts,
 any kind

HOT BUTTERED BOURBON AND CIDER

VEGETARIAN, MAKE AHEAD, QUICK COOKING

Serves 8

6 cups (1.5 L) pressed sweet apple cider

2 cups (500 mL) water

¼ cup (60 mL) packed brown sugar

10 cloves

2 cinnamon sticks (4 inches/10 cm each)

2 strips orange peel, each 2 × ½ inches (5 × 1 cm)

4 tablespoons (60 mL) chilled butter

1 cup (250 mL) bourbon

Juice of 1 lemon

Apple slices, for garnish (optional)

I literally sprint to the calendar on the day I can flip the page from August to September, willing the weather to change and the air to get crisp. It's the time of year I can replace barbecues with braises, surround myself with baskets of Honeycrisps and Galas from the farmers' market, and coerce the kids into taking a picture, or ten, at the pumpkin patch. We also spend a lot of time sipping cider in the fall, and this spiked version is one we like to serve at Thanksgiving and Halloween.

1. In a medium Dutch oven (4 to 6 quarts/3.8 to 5.7 L), combine the apple cider, water, brown sugar, cloves, cinnamon, and orange peel and bring to a simmer over medium-high heat. Reduce the heat to low, cover, and let steep for 20 minutes.

2. Add the chilled butter to the pot and increase the heat to return the liquid to a simmer. Stir in the bourbon and lemon juice. Strain into a pitcher or large glass measuring cup. Divide between mugs and top with an apple slice sprinkled with cinnamon and nutmeg, if using.

HONEY CARDAMOM STEAMERS

Serves 2

Hot drinks are often associated with *hygge*, that ubiquitous Danish word for getting cozy. This one in particular is especially comforting and can ease you into a relaxed state before bed, or anytime you need to de-stress. Steamers are essentially nothing more than a glass of warm, lightly flavoured milk whizzed up a little with a frothing wand or immersion blender. Ideal for the little ones in your life, the honey and spice infusion in this drink is less sweet than hot chocolate and contains no caffeine.

2 cups (500 mL) milk (any kind)

2 tablespoons (30 mL) liquid honey, plus extra for drizzling (optional)

½ teaspoon (2 mL) vanilla bean paste or pure vanilla extract

½ teaspoon (2 mL) ground cardamom, plus extra for serving

1. In a medium Dutch oven (4 to 6 quarts/3.8 to 5.7 L), heat the milk over medium heat until warm and steamy, with bubbles forming around the perimeter of the pot, about 5 minutes. Stir in the honey, vanilla, and cardamom.
2. Immerse a frothing wand in the milk and turn it on. Whisk, creating a swirl of milk, until frothed to your liking. If you don't have a frothing wand, you can use a handheld immersion blender to create the desired frothiness.
3. Divide the milk evenly between 2 cups and drizzle with extra honey, if using. Sprinkle with cardamom and serve immediately.

RICH HOT CHOCOLATE

VEGETARIAN, KID FRIENDLY, QUICK COOKING, GLUTEN-FREE

Serves 4

¾ cup (175 mL) water

3 tablespoons (45 mL) cocoa powder

4 cups (1 L) milk

4 ounces (110 g) semi-sweet or dark chocolate, finely chopped

1 to 2 tablespoons (15 to 30 mL) packed brown sugar

Optional toppings for serving: cold whipped cream, marshmallows, chocolate sauce, chocolate sprinkles

When the mornings turn cold, this drink becomes part of our daily breakfast routine. I blame it on the time I lived in the south of France, where it was common practice for children to drink this beverage every morning. I skip the marshmallows and whipped cream if this drink is a part of our morning meal, but when we sip it after school or on the weekends, there is no limit to the selection of toppings. We like marshmallows and lightly sweetened whipped cream, not to mention chocolate sauce and sprinkles.

1. In a medium Dutch oven (4 to 6 quarts/3.8 to 5.7 L), bring the water to a boil over medium heat. Whisk in the cocoa powder until no lumps remain. Pour in the milk and return to a simmer, whisking occasionally.
2. Add the chocolate and 1 tablespoon (15 mL) sugar and simmer, whisking frequently, until the chocolate is melted and the mixture is thick and smooth. Taste and add more sugar if you prefer a sweeter drink.
3. Pour the hot chocolate into mugs. Serve at once with your favourite toppings, if using.

TIP: To ensure your hot chocolate stays warm for longer, you can preheat the mugs by filling them with boiling water and then discarding it before pouring in the hot chocolate.

ROOIBOS CHAI TEA LATTE

VEGETARIAN, MAKE AHEAD, KID FRIENDLY,
QUICK COOKING, GLUTEN-FREE

Serves 4

Made from a South African plant, rooibos (pronounced ROY-bos) tea is an antioxidant-filled, caffeine-free tea that is perfect to pour for both kids and adults alike. When infused with classic chai spices like ginger, cardamom, and cloves, it quickly transforms into the fuzzy blanket of hot breakfast drinks. I like to serve mine in latte form, with steamed milk and honey, but you can sip it as is, if desired. If you can't locate loose leaf rooibos tea, feel free to use the bagged variety instead; you'll need four tea bags for four lattes.

1. In a medium Dutch oven (4 to 6 quarts/3.8 to 5.7 L), combine the cardamom pods, cloves, star anise, peppercorns, cinnamon, ginger, tea, and water. Bring to a boil, reduce heat to medium-low, and simmer for 4 to 6 minutes or until very fragrant.
2. Strain the tea into 4 mugs. Stir in the milk and honey, sprinkle with ground cinnamon and top with a star of anise if desired, and serve hot.

VARIATION: To make an iced rooibos chai tea latte, prepare the tea as instructed in step 1. Strain into a heatproof pitcher and chill thoroughly in the fridge. To serve, pour tea into ice-filled glasses and stir in cold milk of choice and agave nectar, to taste.

12 whole green cardamom pods

12 whole cloves

4 star anise

4 black peppercorns

1 cinnamon stick (about 4 inches/ 10 cm)

1 piece fresh ginger (about 1 inch/ 2.5 cm), peeled

4 tablespoons (60 mL) loose leaf rooibos tea

4 cups (1 L) water

1 cup (250 mL) hot, frothed, or steamed milk

Liquid honey, to taste

For serving (optional)

Ground cinnamon

Star anise

SPECIAL OCCASIONS MENU PLANNER

I worked in catering for many years, and without question my favourite part of the job was helping people plan their party menus. It was like putting together a delicious puzzle, making sure that flavours weren't repeated too frequently, a variety of textures were included, and seasonal ingredients appeared as often as possible. I've put my party-planning hat back on here, providing you with a list of recipes from within these pages that could be used for your own special occasions. Almost all of these menus could benefit from the addition of a light green salad or a platter of crudités, which I definitely recommend serving with the Roasted Red Onion Party Dip (page 239).

KID'S BIRTHDAY PARTY

Baked Mozzarella Sticks (page 241)

Macaroni and Cheese (cheddar cheese variation)
(page 163)

Single Layer Chocolate Celebration Cake
(page 220)

TEENAGER'S BIRTHDAY PARTY

Salami Stromboli (page 110)

Spinach and Ricotta Wonton Mini
Lasagnas (page 159)

Individual Mocha Molten Cakes (page 229)

GIRLS' NIGHT IN

Cream of Mushroom Soup with Mustard and
Lemon (page 59)

Roasted Lentil and Walnut Salad with Grapes,
Spinach, and Goat Cheese (page 182)

Grilled Apple and Brie Sandwiches (page 99)

Salted Chocolate Tahini Skillet Blondies (page 210)

COMFORT FOOD DINNER

One-Pot Baked Beefaroni (page 142)

Cheesy Garlic and Green Onion Pull-Apart Bread
(page 84)

Fudgy Raspberry Swirl Brownies (page 206)

SLEEPOVER BREAKFAST

Overnight French Toast Casserole
(page 35)

Spicy Corn and Bacon Frittata (page 21)

Spiced Pumpkin Quinoa Muffins (page 40)

Rich Hot Chocolate (page 258)

SUMMER PARTY MENU

Stovetop Shrimp Boil (page 149)

Honey, Thyme, and Cheddar Skillet Cornbread
(page 83)

Rustic Stone Fruit Crostata with Cornmeal Crust
(page 217)

DATE NIGHT

Cider-Braised Mussels with Mustard and Cream
(page 145)

Overnight Faux Sourdough (page 80)

Fudgy Raspberry Swirl Brownies (page 206)

CASUAL WEEKNIGHT DINNER

Mixed Olives with Chorizo and Almonds
(page 242)

One-Pan Paella (page 126)

Single Layer Chocolate Celebration Cake
(page 220)

GAME DAY GATHERING

Buffalo Chicken and Blue Cheese–Stuffed Celery
    Sticks (page 240)
Barbecue Chickpea Pizza (page 104)
Pork and Green Salsa Chili (page 71)
Ice Cream Cone Pie (page 226)
Pretzel Magic Bars (page 209)

HOLIDAY HAPPY HOUR

Hot Buttered Bourbon and Cider (page 254)
Mixed Olives with Chorizo and Almonds
    (page 242)
Warm Artichoke, Kale, and White
    Bean Dip (page 236)
Jalapeño Popper Rolls (page 91)

VEGETARIAN DINNER

Roasted Lentil and Walnut Salad with Grapes,
    Spinach, and Goat Cheese (page 182)
Samosa Skillet Pot Pie with Minted Yogurt Sauce
    (page 155)
Fall Fruit Crisp (page 223)

SYMPATHY MEAL PACKAGE

Flat Roasted Chicken with Farro (page 123)
Caldo Verde (page 63)
Overnight Faux Sourdough (page 80)
Spiced Cocoa Molasses Cookies (page 202)

WINTER SUNDAY SUPPER

Mixed Olives with Chorizo and Almonds
    (page 242)
Oven-Baked Balsamic Beef and
    Vegetable Stew (page 75)
Lemon Pudding Cake (page 213)
Honey Cardamom Steamers (page 257)

SPRING SUNDAY SUPPER

Skillet Gnocchi with Bacon and Peas (page 156)
Cheesy Garlic and Green Onion Pull-Apart Bread
    (page 84)
Maple Walnut Biscotti (page 205)
Rooibos Chai Tea Latte (page 261)

SUMMER SUNDAY SUPPER

Perfect Saucy Pulled Pork (page 134)
Sweet and Saucy Baked Beans (page 191)
Quick Cabbage Slaw (page 113)
Quick Pickled Jalapeños (page 248)
Triple Berry Crumb Bars (page 225)

FALL SUNDAY SUPPER

Barbecue Chicken Chili with Cornbread
    Dumplings (page 72)
Harvest Kale Platter Salad (page 172)
Sour Cream Apple Slab Pie (page 215)

FIND IT FAST: RECIPE INDEX BY VESSEL

SHEET PAN

Baked Beef Kofta with Lemon Parsley Couscous (page 141)

Baked Mozzarella Sticks (page 241)

Barbecue Chickpea Pizza (page 104)

Brown Sugar and Chili–Rubbed Salmon Sheet Pan Dinner (page 146)

Cheesy Garlic and Green Onion Pull-Apart Bread (page 84)

Chili-Lime Potato Nachos (page 151)

Crispy Cauliflower with Raisins, Capers, and Lemony Bread Crumbs (page 171)

Crispy Chicken Sandwiches (page 96)

Easy Grilled Cheese for a Crowd (page 95)

Golden Apricot Granola (page 36)

Harvest Kale Platter Salad (page 172)

Maple Walnut Biscotti (page 205)

Peach, Prosciutto, and Brie Flatbread (page 103)

Pecan Sandie Spelt Scones (page 39)

Pork Tenderloin with Root Vegetables and Herby Dipping Sauce (page 138)

Roasted Corn on the Cob with Herb Butter (page 179)

Roasted Red Onion Party Dip (page 239)

Roasted Sheet Pan Chicken with Potatoes, Cauliflower, and Olives (page 129)

Rustic Stone Fruit Crostata with Cornmeal Crust (page 217)

Salami Stromboli (page 110)

Sheet Pan Breakfast with Sweet Potatoes and Chickpeas (page 30)

Sheet Pan Sausages with Peppers and Polenta (page 137)

Sour Cream Apple Slab Pie (page 215)

Spiced Cocoa Molasses Cookies (page 202)

Toasted Nuts, Two Ways (page 253)

BAKING PAN

Almond Butter and Jam Breakfast Bars (page 43)

Baked Apple Spice Doughnuts (page 198)

Baked Oatmeal and Pear Breakfast Pie with Walnut Streusel Topping (page 22)

Carrot Cake Snacking Loaf with Cream Cheese Frosting (page 201)

Fudgy Raspberry Swirl Brownies (page 206)

Goat Cheese and Dill Hash Brown Quiche (page 29)

Ice Cream Cone Pie (page 226)

Individual Mocha Molten Cakes (page 229)

Jalapeño Popper Rolls (page 91)

Melt-in-Your-Mouth Potatoes (page 180)

Muffin Pan Tuna Melts (page 107)

Pretzel Magic Bars (page 209)

Simple Meat-Lover's Deep-Dish Pizza (page 109)

Single Layer Chocolate Celebration Cake (page 220)

Spiced Pumpkin Quinoa Muffins (page 40)

Spinach and Ricotta Wonton Mini Lasagnas (page 159)

Triple Berry Crumb Bars (page 225)

CASSEROLE DISH

Buffalo Chicken and Blue Cheese–Stuffed Celery Sticks (page 240)

Coconut Rice with Hoisin-Glazed Turkey Meatballs (page 130)

Crowd-Pleasing Puffy Oven Pancake (page 25)

Four Season Fruit Crisp (page 223)

Ham and Cheese Croissant Casserole (page 33)

Lemon Pudding Cake (page 213)

Mini Cubano Sandwiches (page 93)

Oven-Baked Balsamic Beef and Vegetable Stew (page 75)

Simple Scalloped Potatoes with Celeriac (page 186)

Twice-Baked Butternut Squash (page 192)

Warm Artichoke, Kale, and White Bean Dip (page 236)

WITH THANKS

I've spent the past four years writing two books, birthing one baby, raising two other children, and researching, writing, and editing 732 freelance articles and recipes (I counted them for the purpose of these acknowledgements). I haven't had nearly enough showers, I've been impossibly sleep deprived, and I don't wear a wireless activity tracker because I prefer to live in denial about the lack of steps I've taken over the previous 1460 days. While it may sound impressive, the reality is that everything I've accomplished is because of the wisdom, guidance, friendship, assistance, support, kindness, and love of so many other people. I've been lucky enough to stand on the shoulders of those who are smarter and better than me to make a few of my own personal dreams come true, and for that I'm so very thankful.

To Carly Watters: Working with you has been everything I ever hoped for in a business partnership: collaborative, fun, and successful! Thank you for taking a chance and adding me to your team of awe-inspiring writers and for believing I could write whatever project came our way.

To Rachel Brown, Laura Dosky, Andrea Magyar, and the Penguin team: Thank you for your tireless enthusiasm, thoughtful feedback, and belief that I could tackle this project. I'm so grateful to have you all in my corner.

To Jennifer Bartoli: You exude class, grace, kindness, and patience, not to mention heaps of style, and this book immediately got better when you agreed to work on it with me. Thank you.

To my recipe testers: Robyn, Julie, Meaghan, Tess, Carly, Beth, Shannon, Mom, Jenn (and those who preferred not to be named), thank you for your time, groceries, feedback, and eagerness to help make these meals taste as good as possible. I really don't think I could have done this without you.

To my family and friends: You are an embarrassment of riches, and there are far too many of you to name individually, but thank you to everyone who taste-tested recipes, held my hand when I thought I might lose it (like during the summer I thought I'd write a book while three kids were home from school), cared for my beloved baby when I needed to work without a toddler hanging off my hips (Mom and Beth, especially), and generally just believed that I was somehow worthy of writing this book. I'm so, so grateful for all of you.

To Benjamin, Jackson, and Matthew Scott: You three are, without any doubt, the greatest gifts of my life and the thing I'm most proud of. The past nineteen years have been a delicious adventure thanks to all of you, and I am forever thankful that my number-one job in this world is to be your mother.

To Rob Scott: There isn't enough space on these pages to thank you for the endless ways in which you love and support me, but you should know that everything about my life got better the minute you walked into it. While I might have guessed that we'd have a family someday, every other amazing adventure with you has been a complete surprise. Thank you for helping to make our marriage so much better than my imagination dreamed it could be.

INDEX